This Journal Belongs To

_____

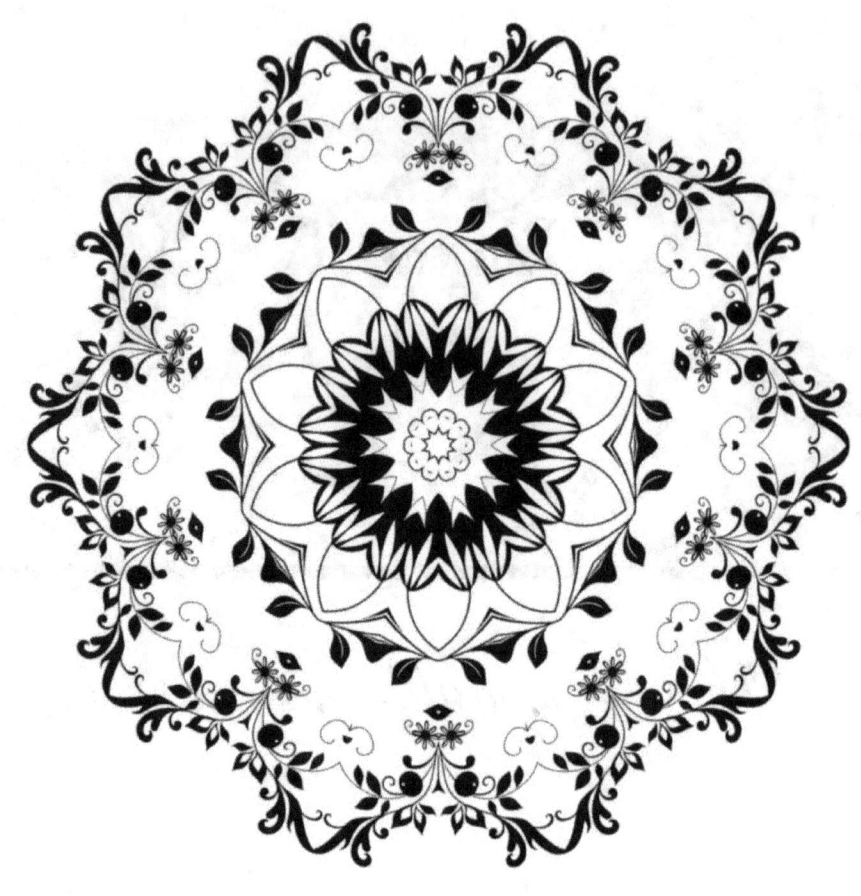

Copyright ©Marcella Mandala Books
All rights reserved.
No part of this book may be reproduced
in any way without permission by the author.

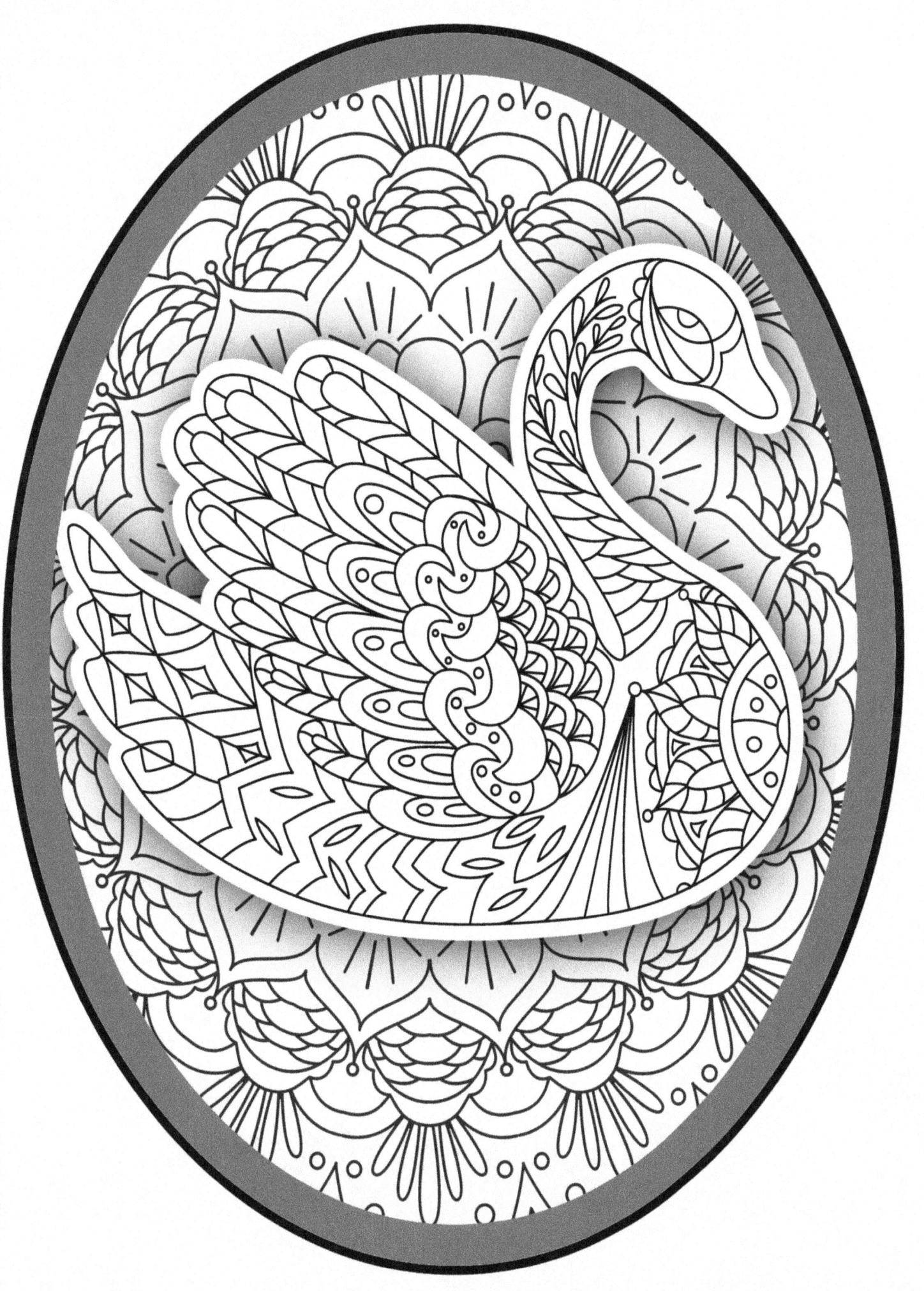

*This page intentionally left blank*

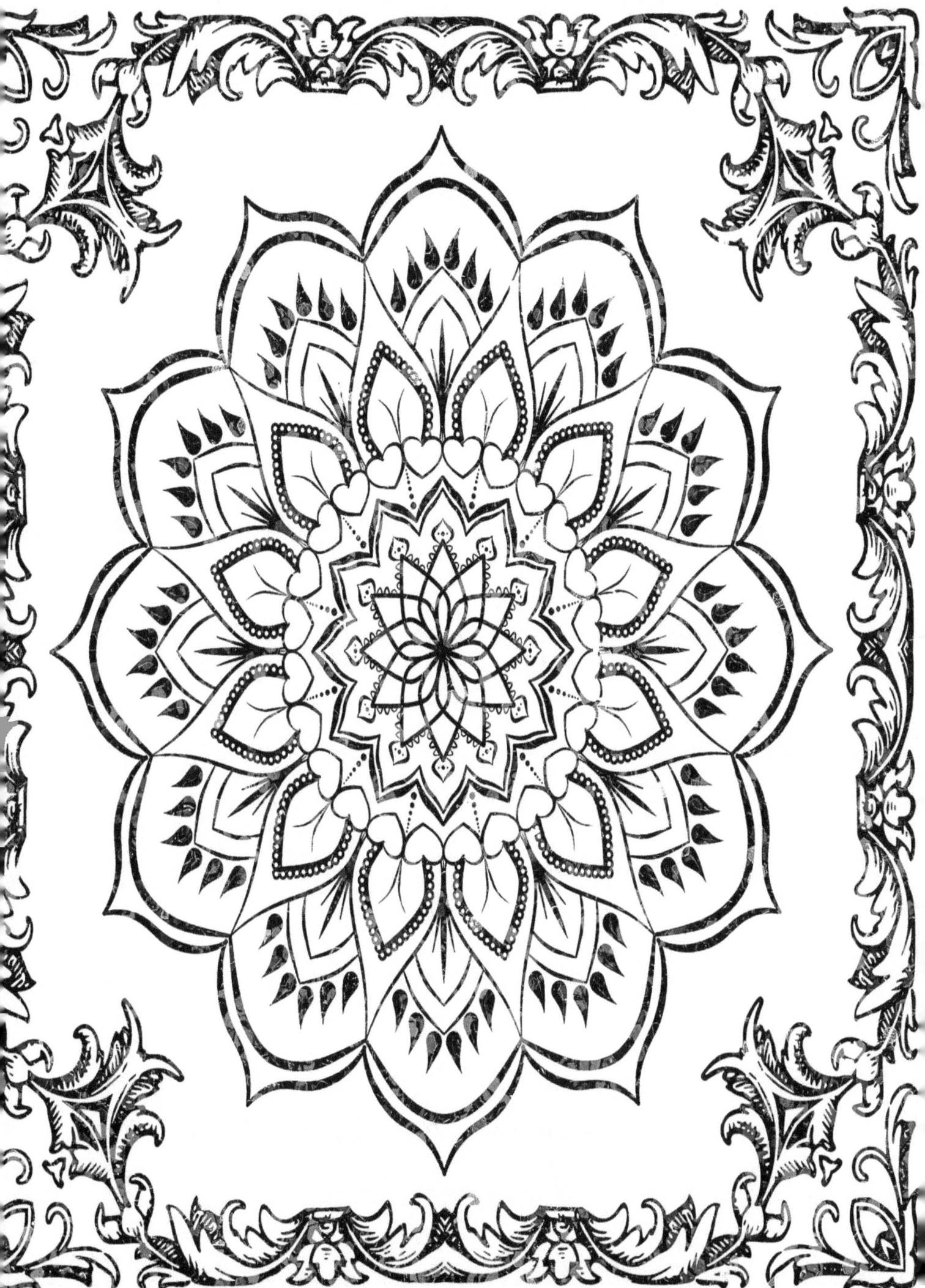

*This page intentionally left blank*

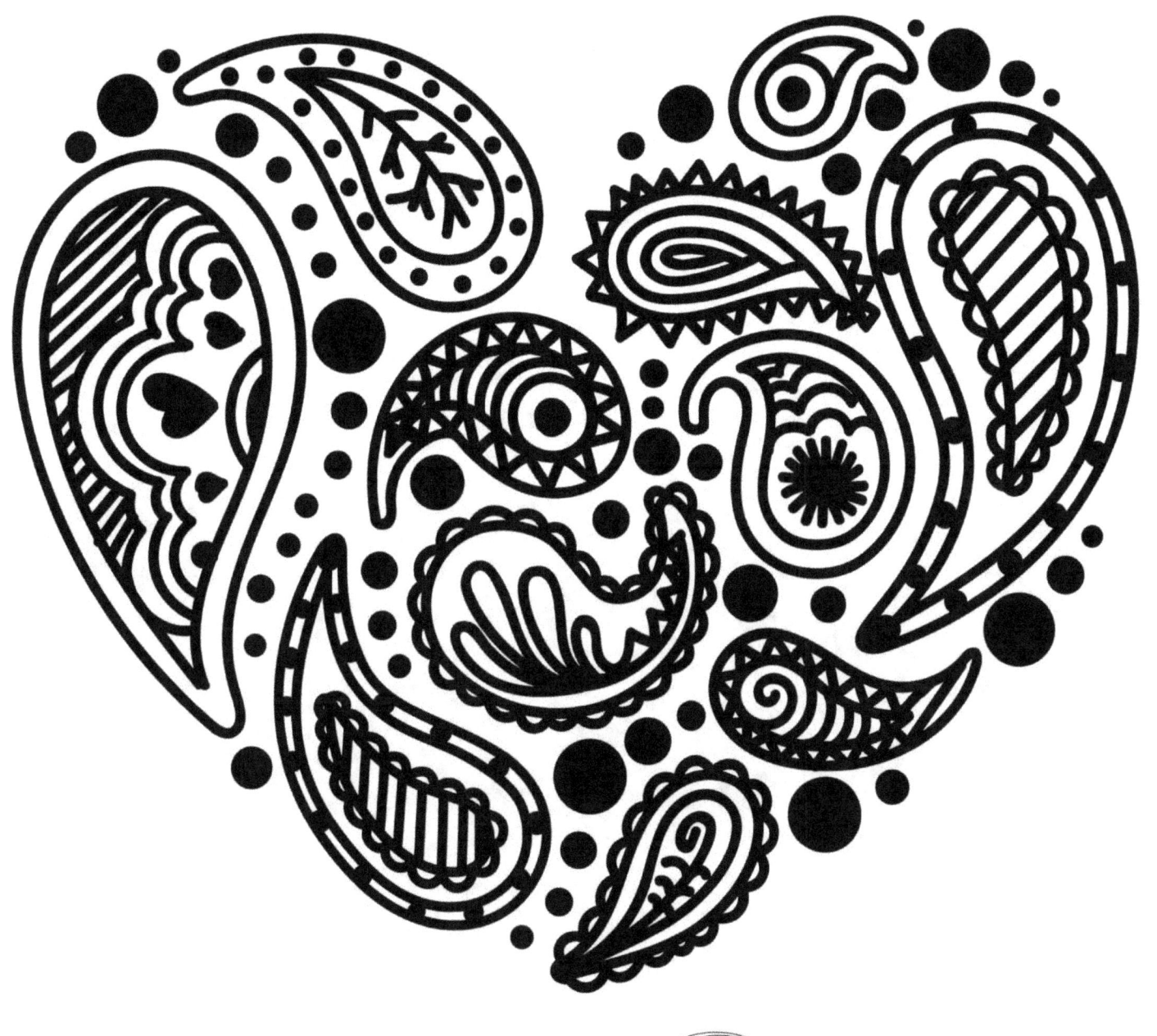

Paisley Heart

*This page intentionally left blank*

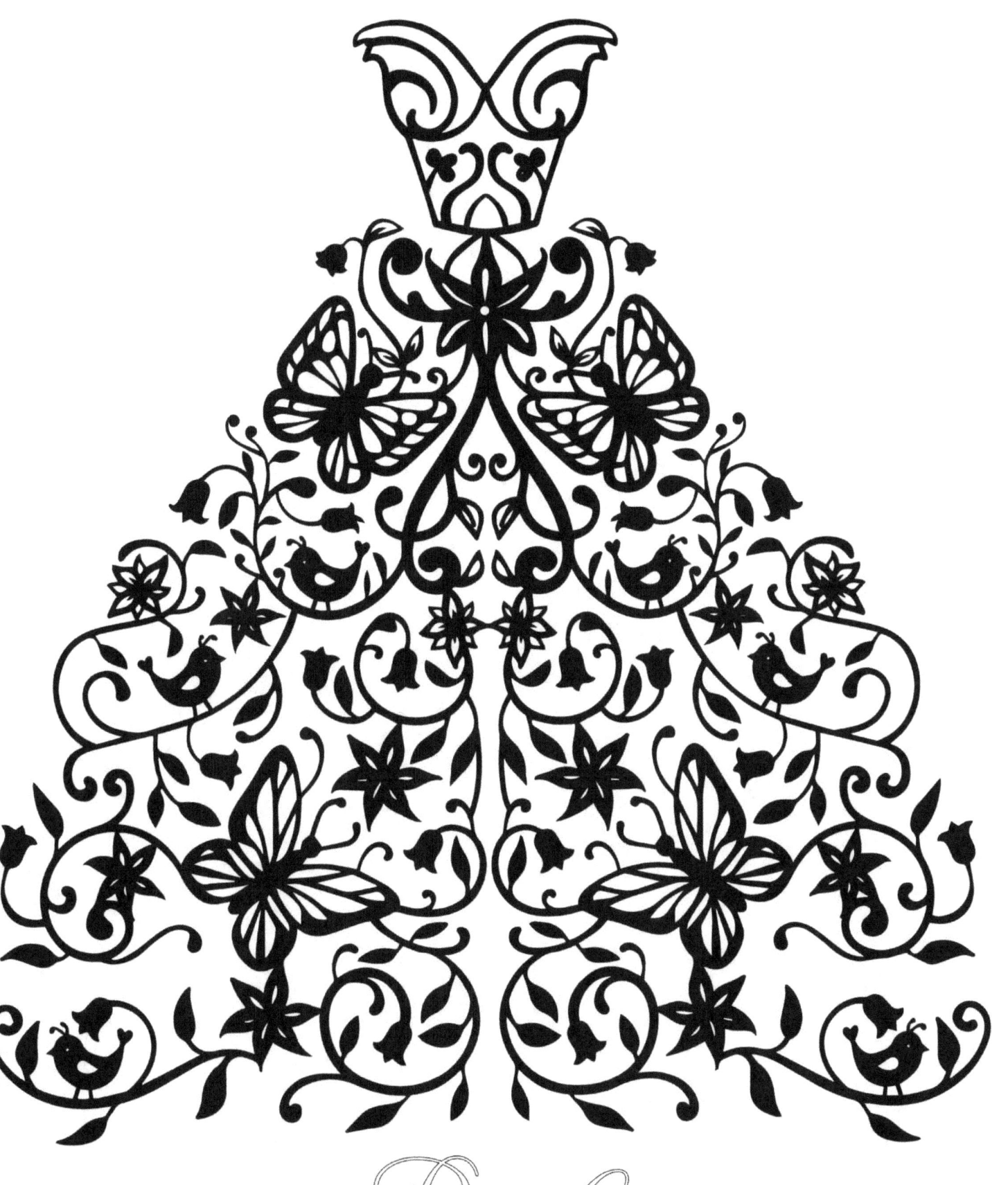

*This page intentionally left blank*

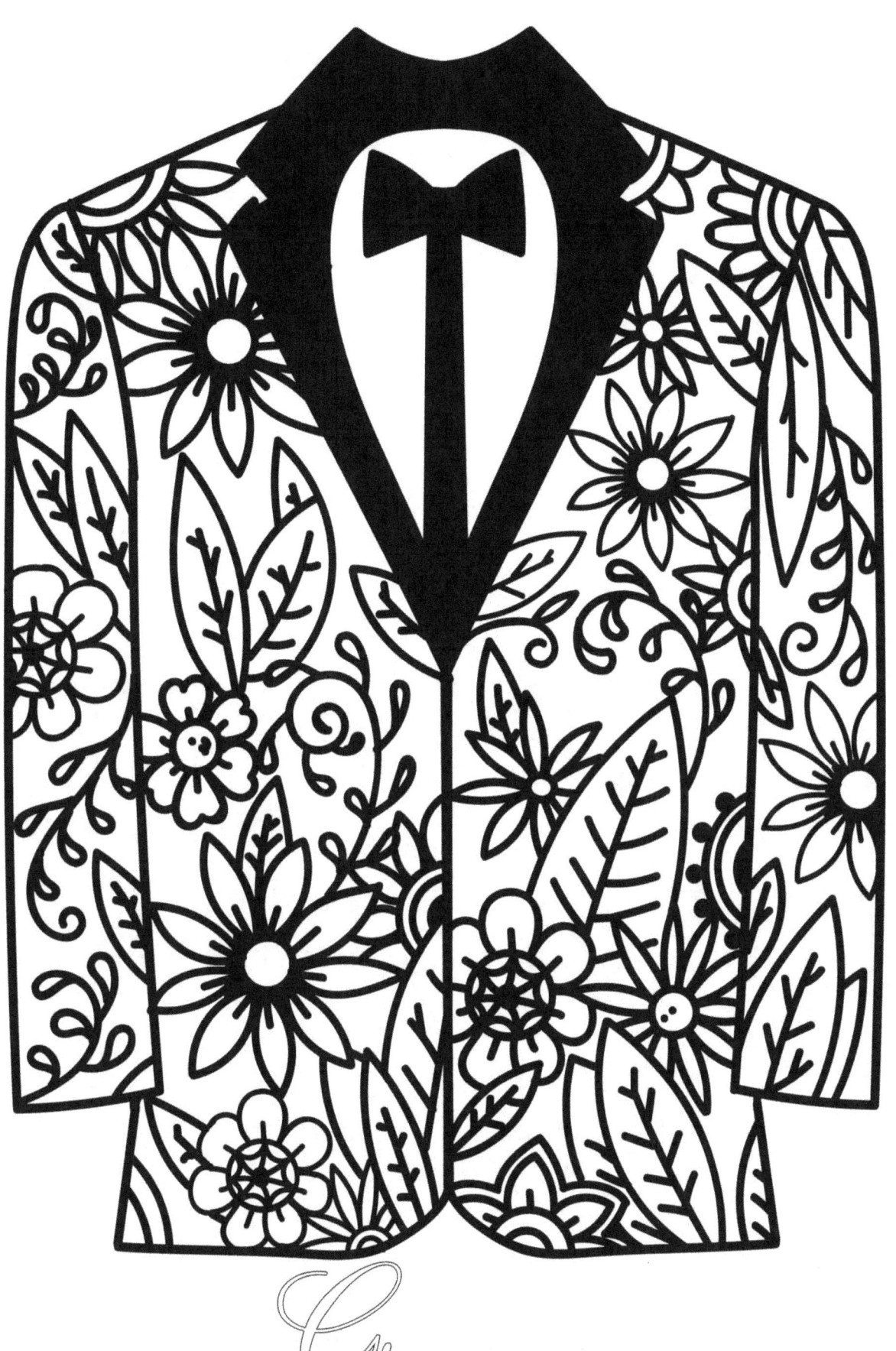

Groom

*This page intentionally left blank*

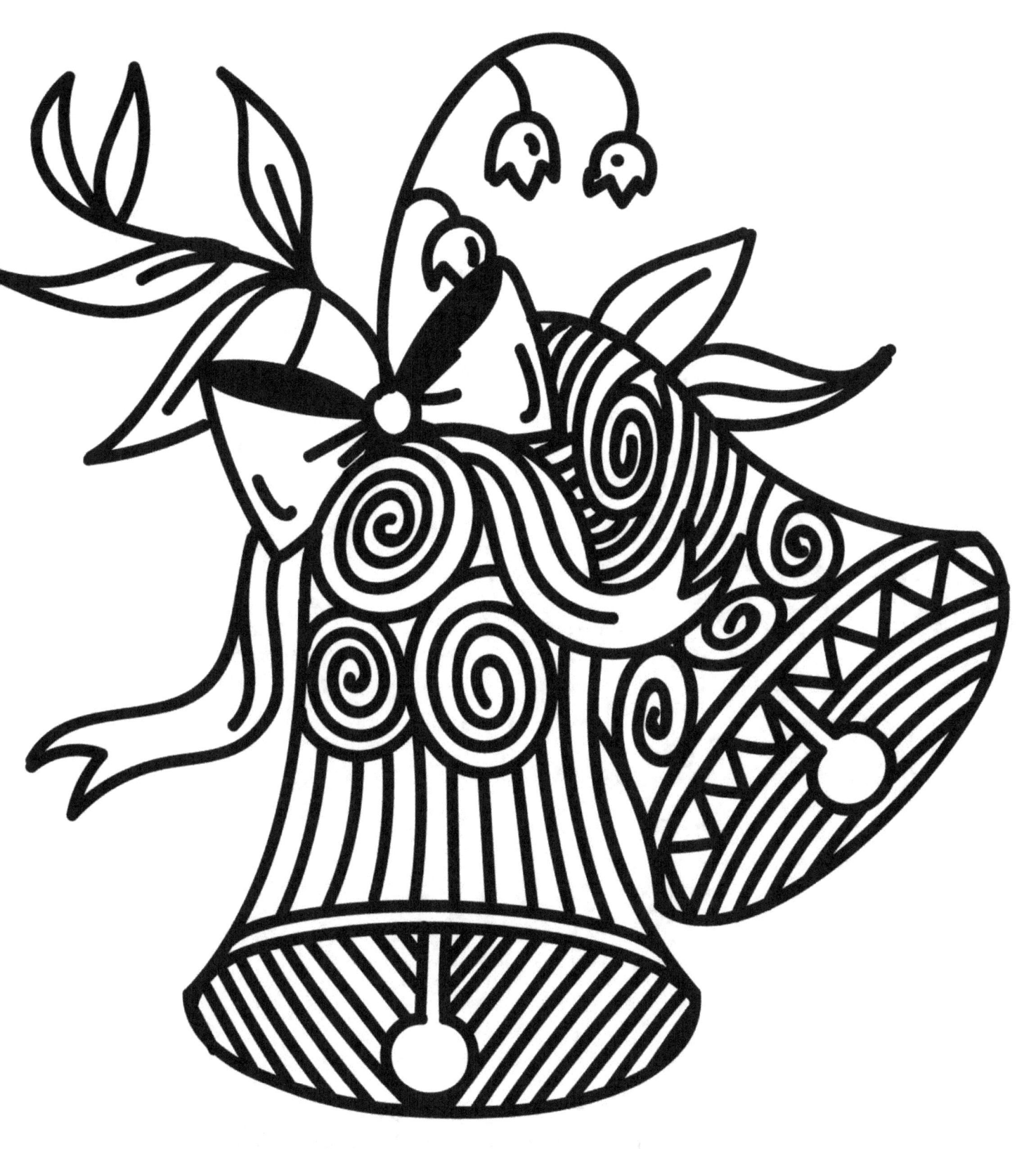

*This page intentionally left blank*

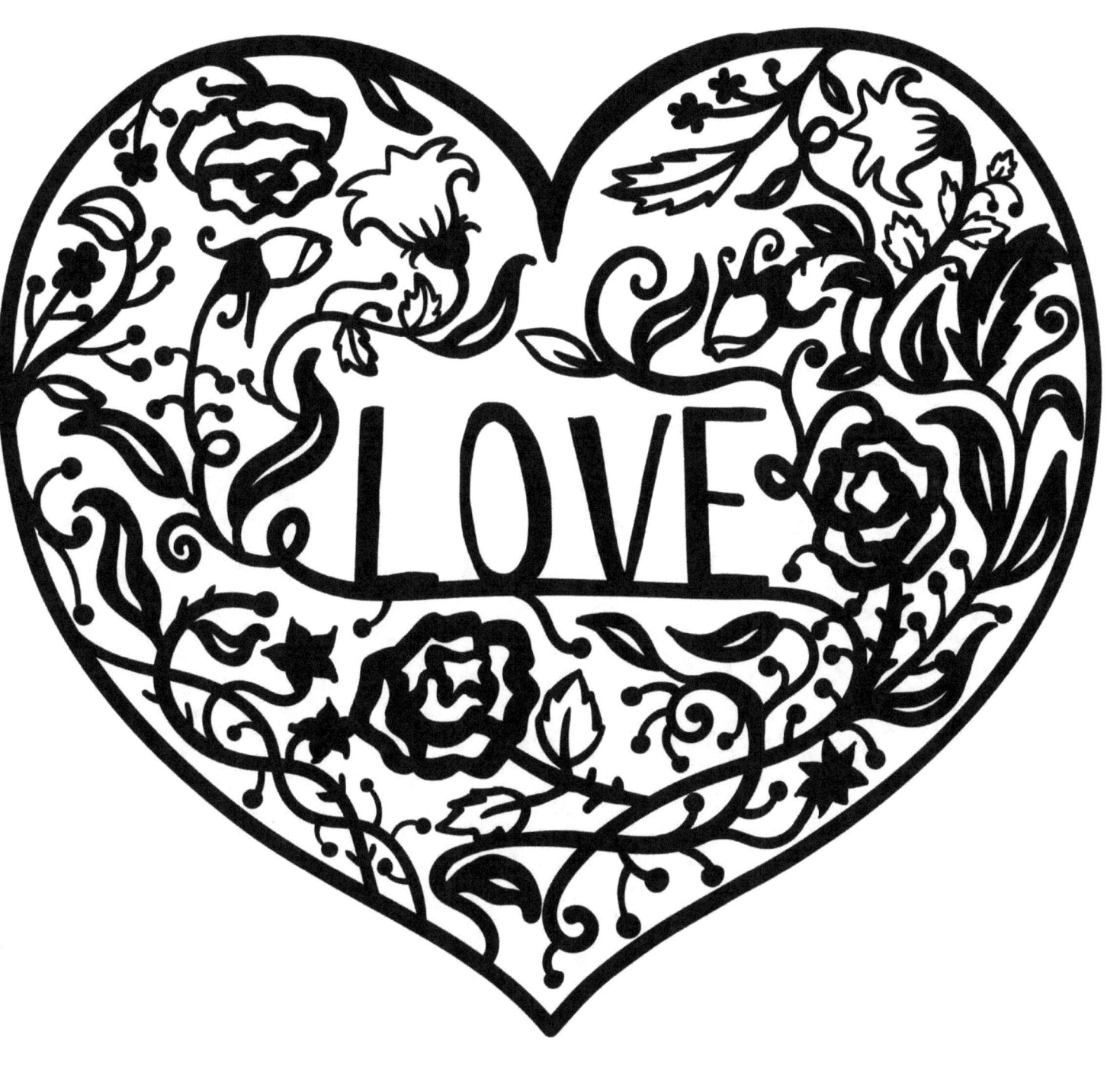

*This page intentionally left blank*

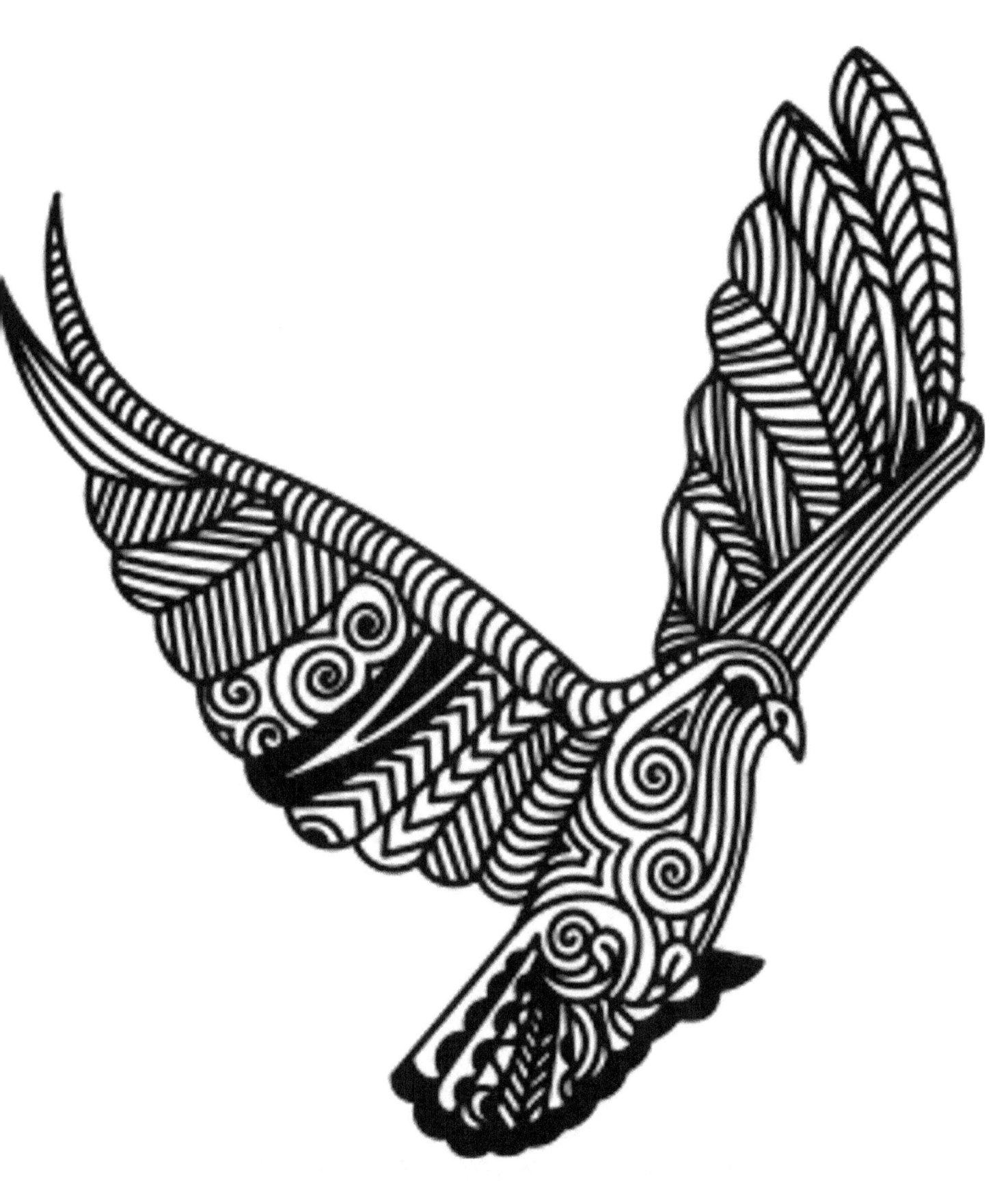

*This page intentionally left blank*

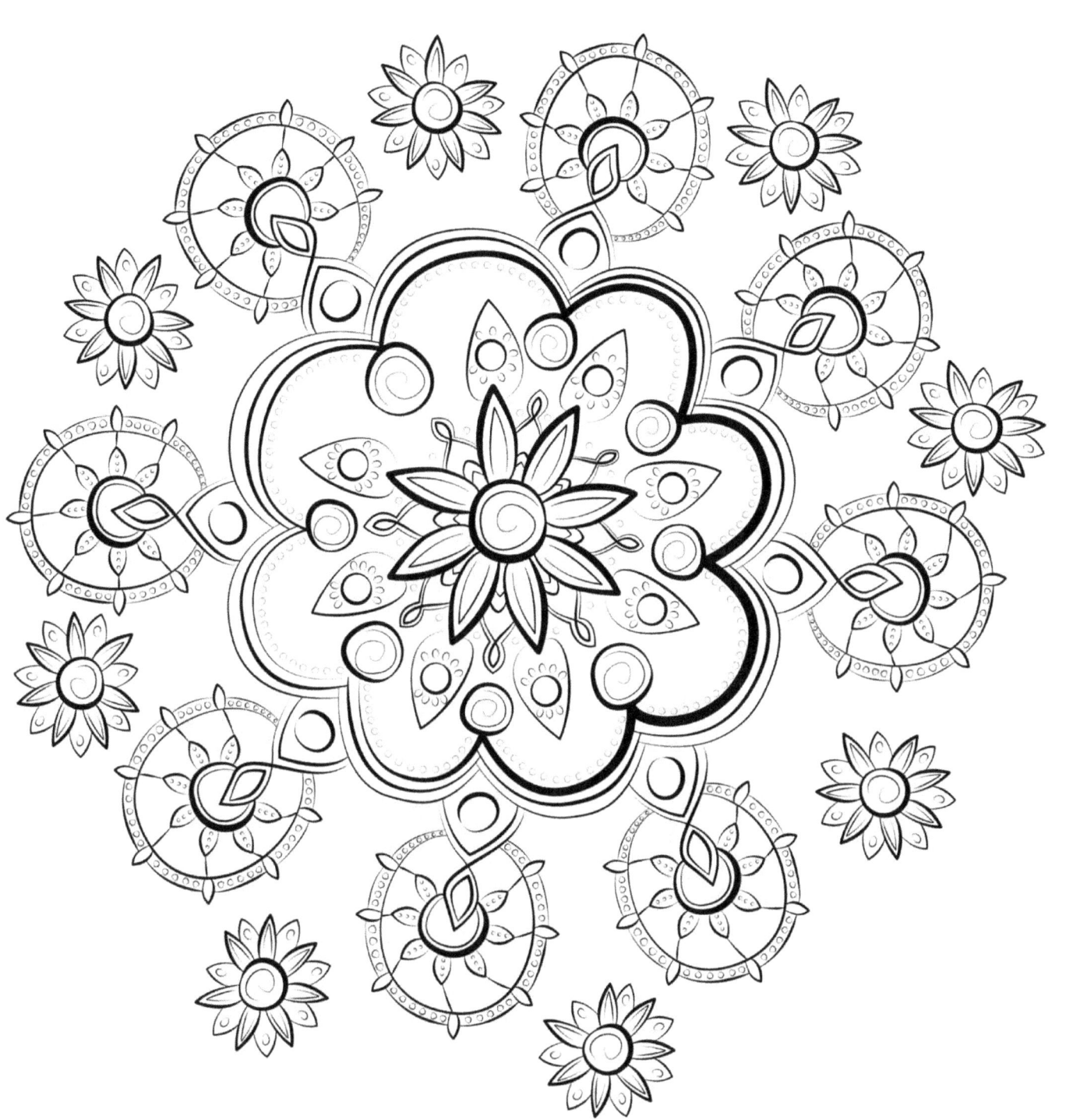

*This page intentionally left blank*

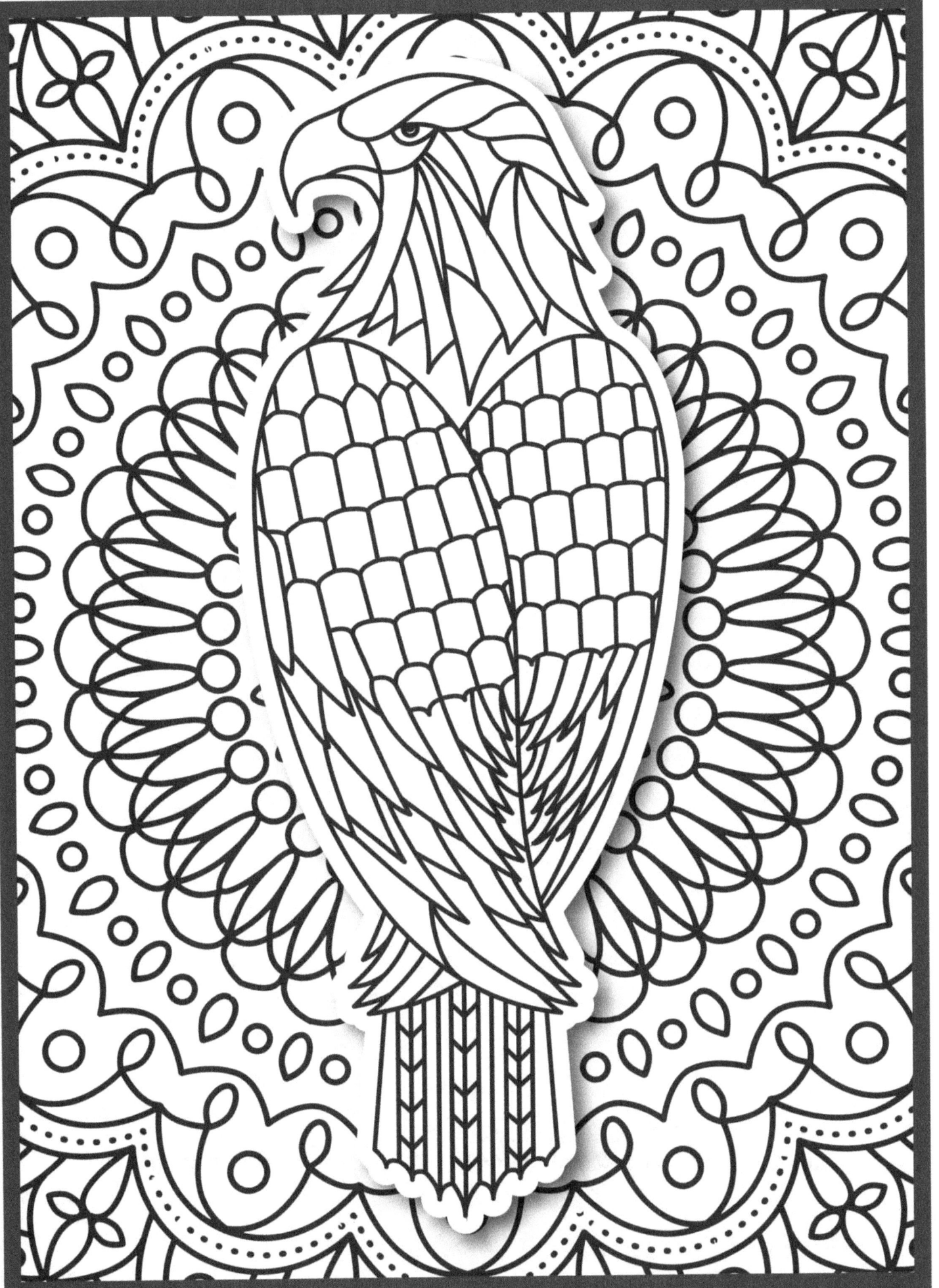

*This page intentionally left blank*

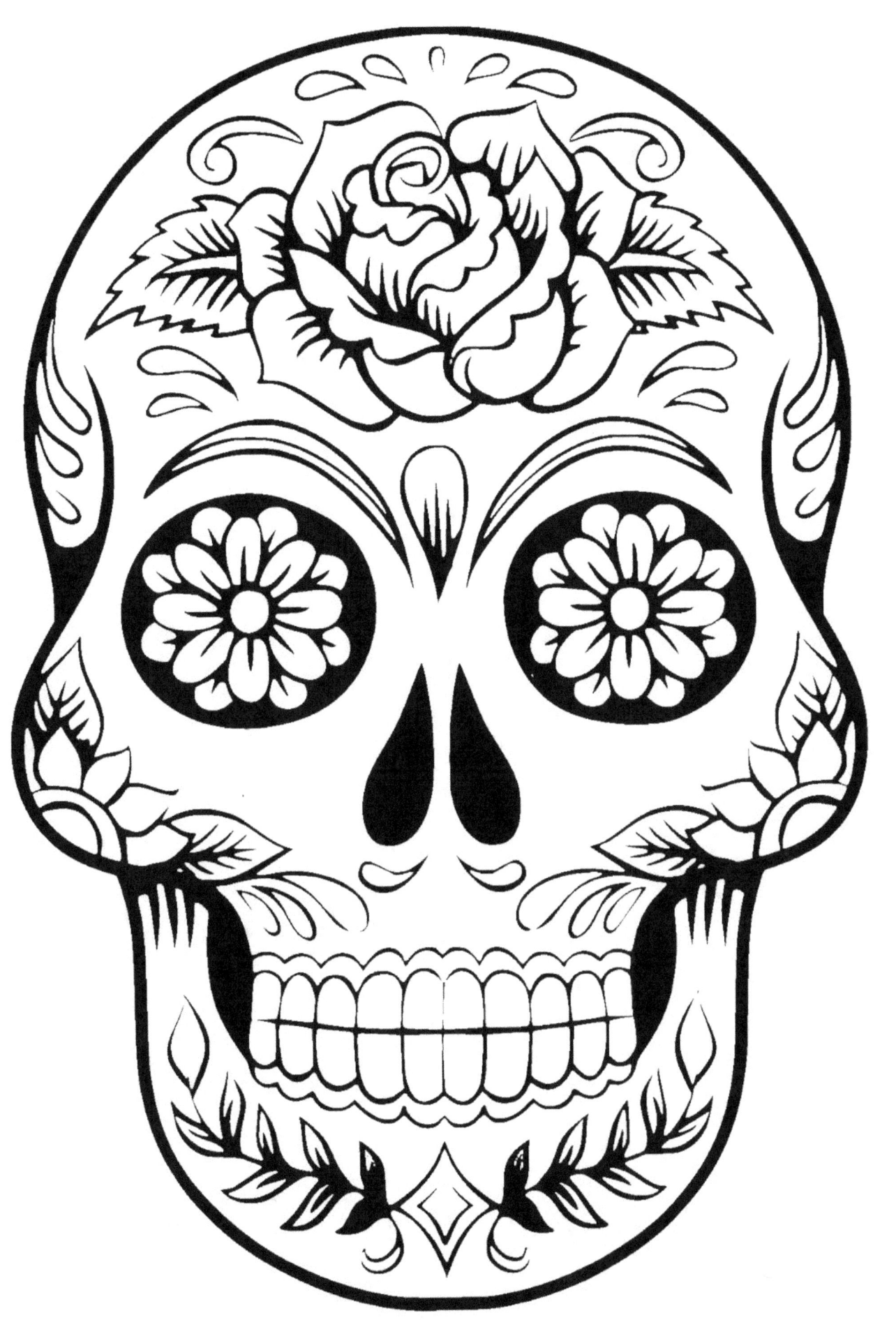

*This page intentionally left blank*

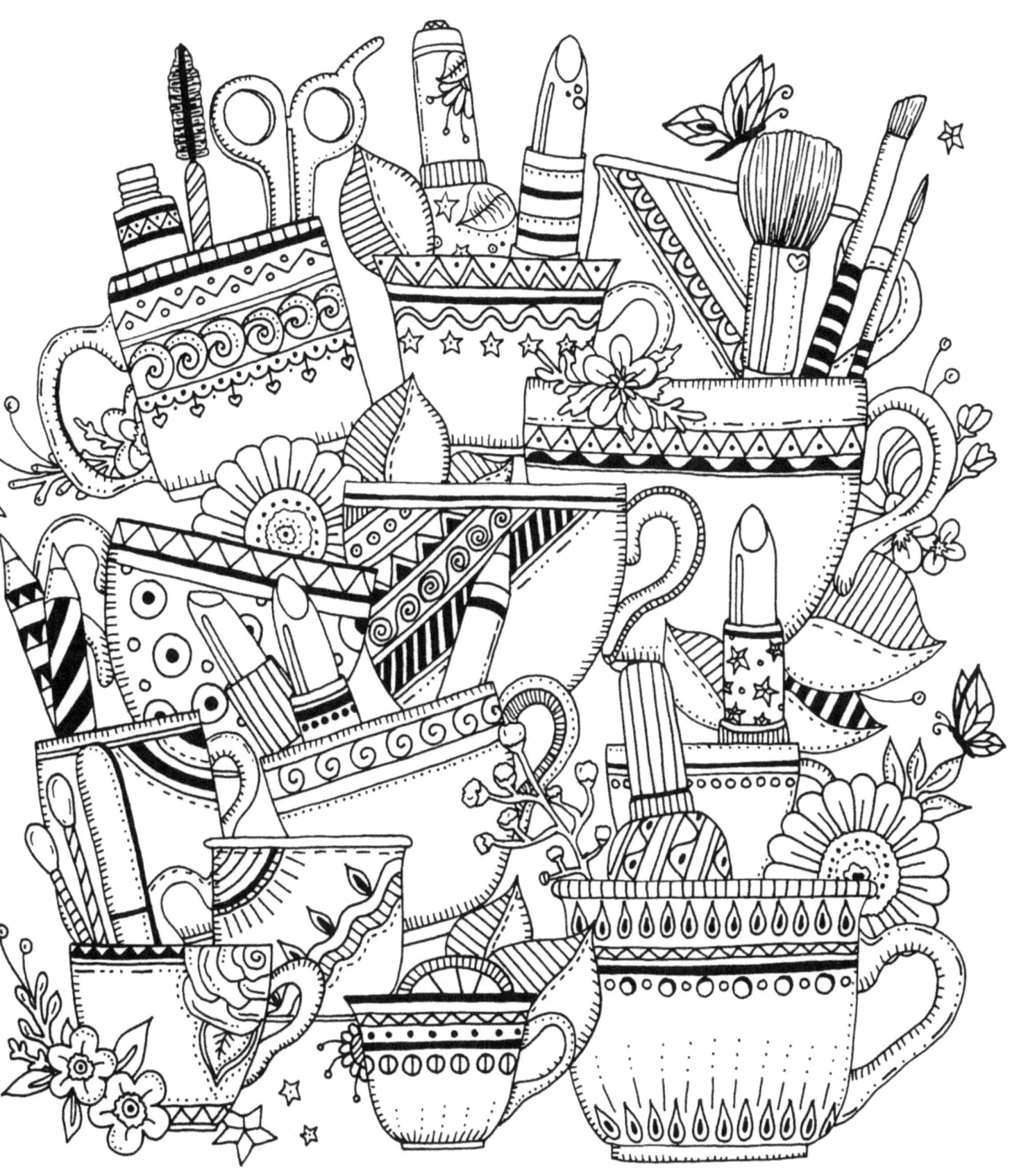

*This page intentionally left blank*

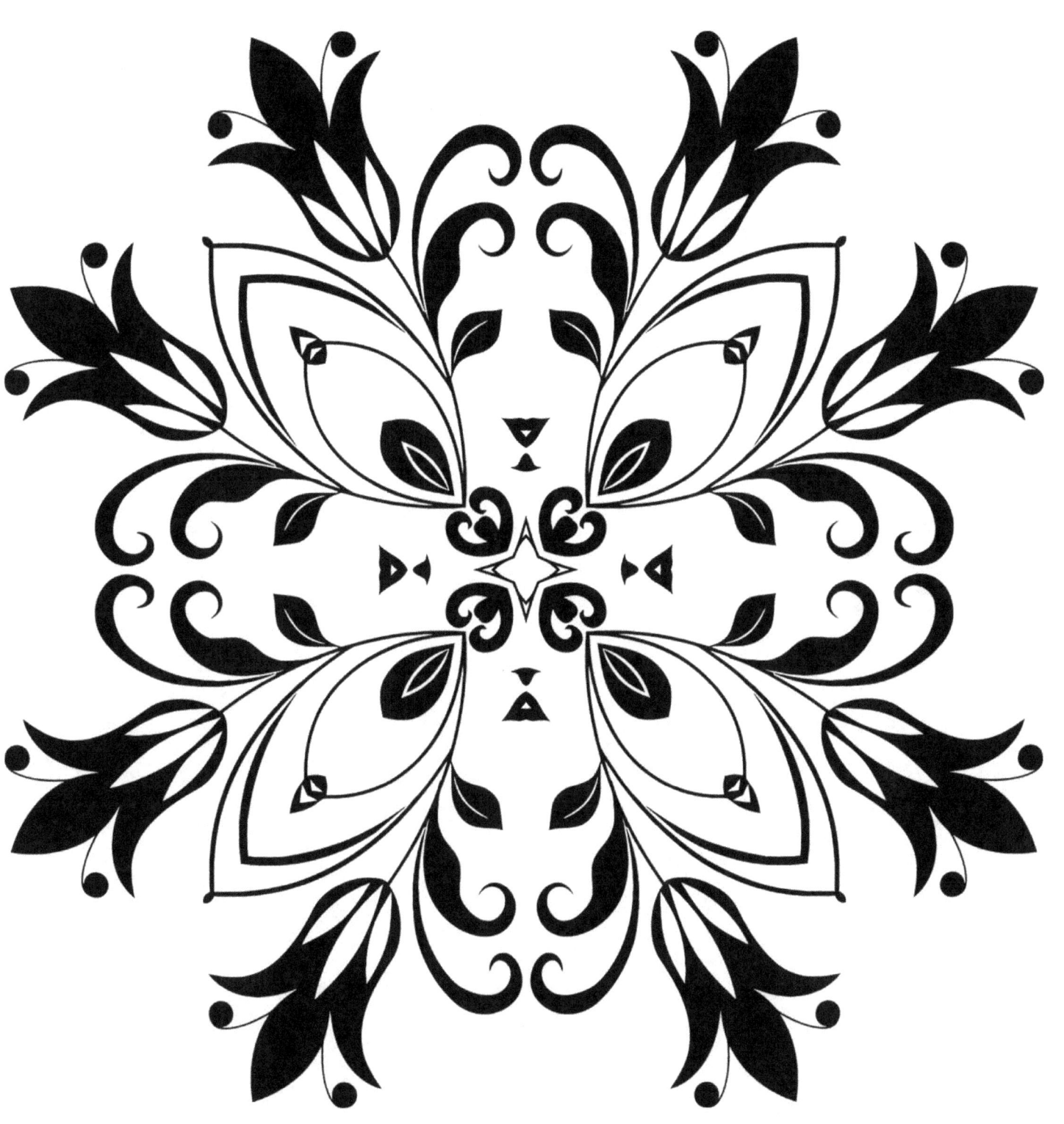

*This page intentionally left blank*

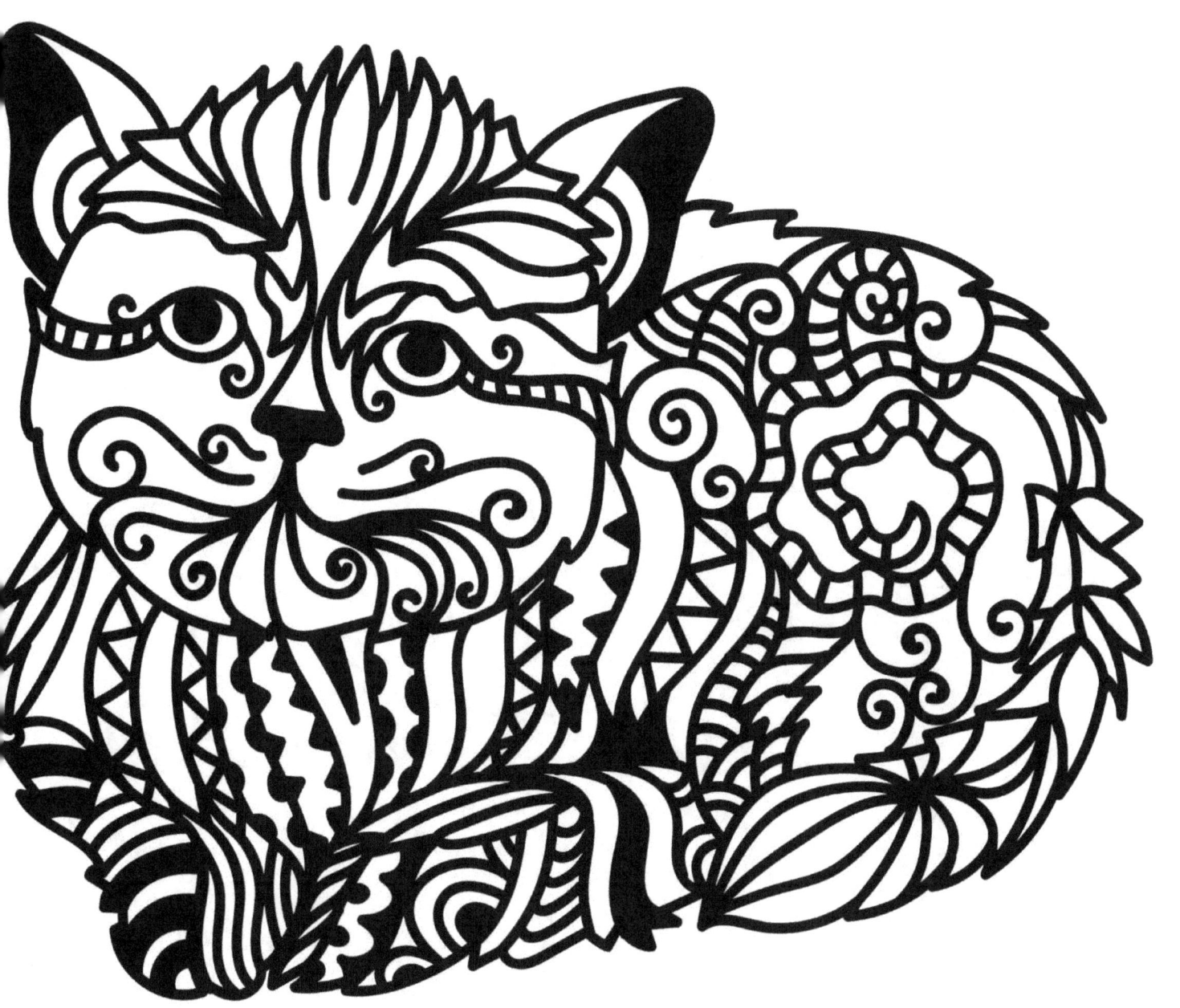

*This page intentionally left blank*

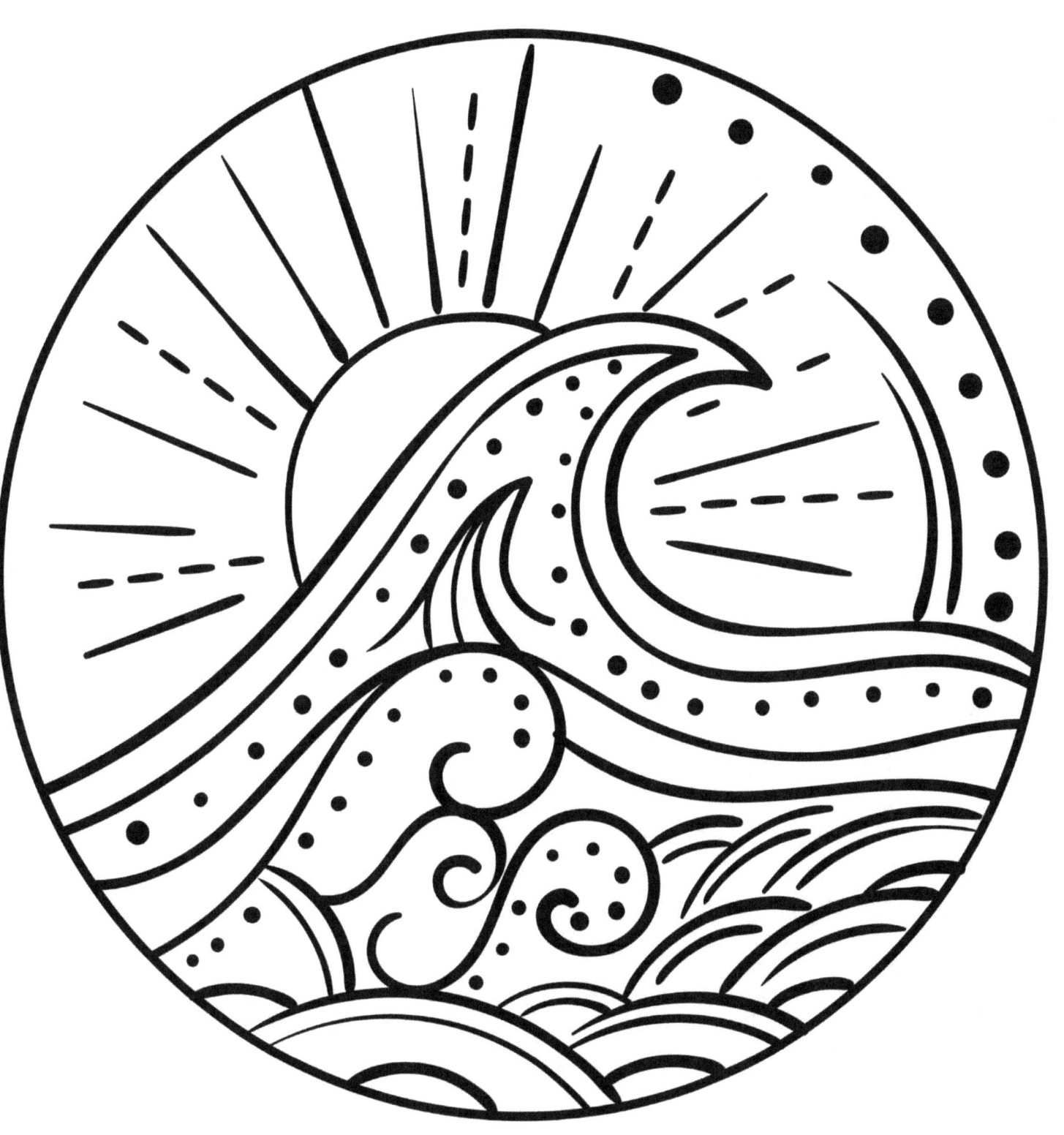

*This page intentionally left blank*

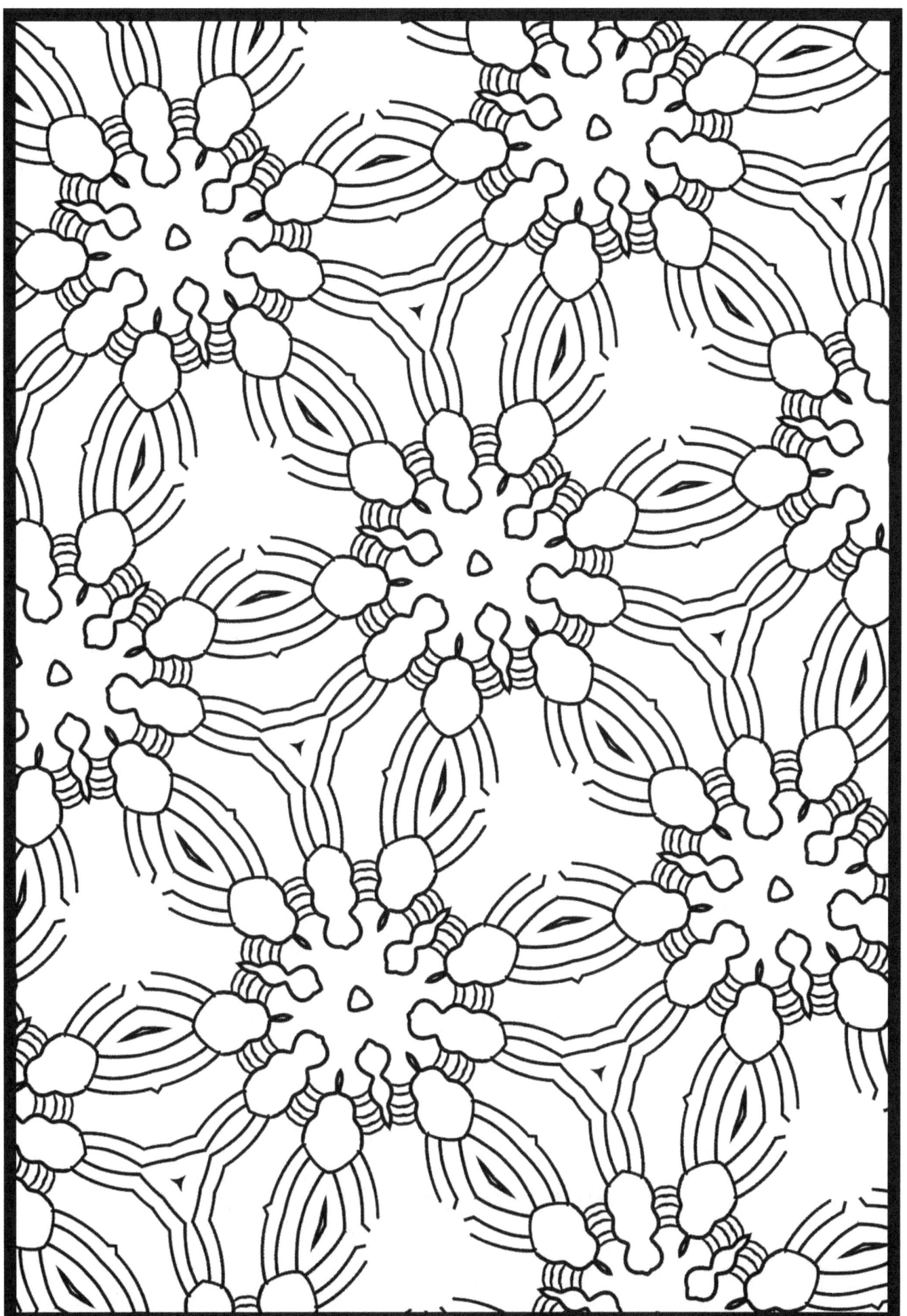

*This page intentionally left blank*

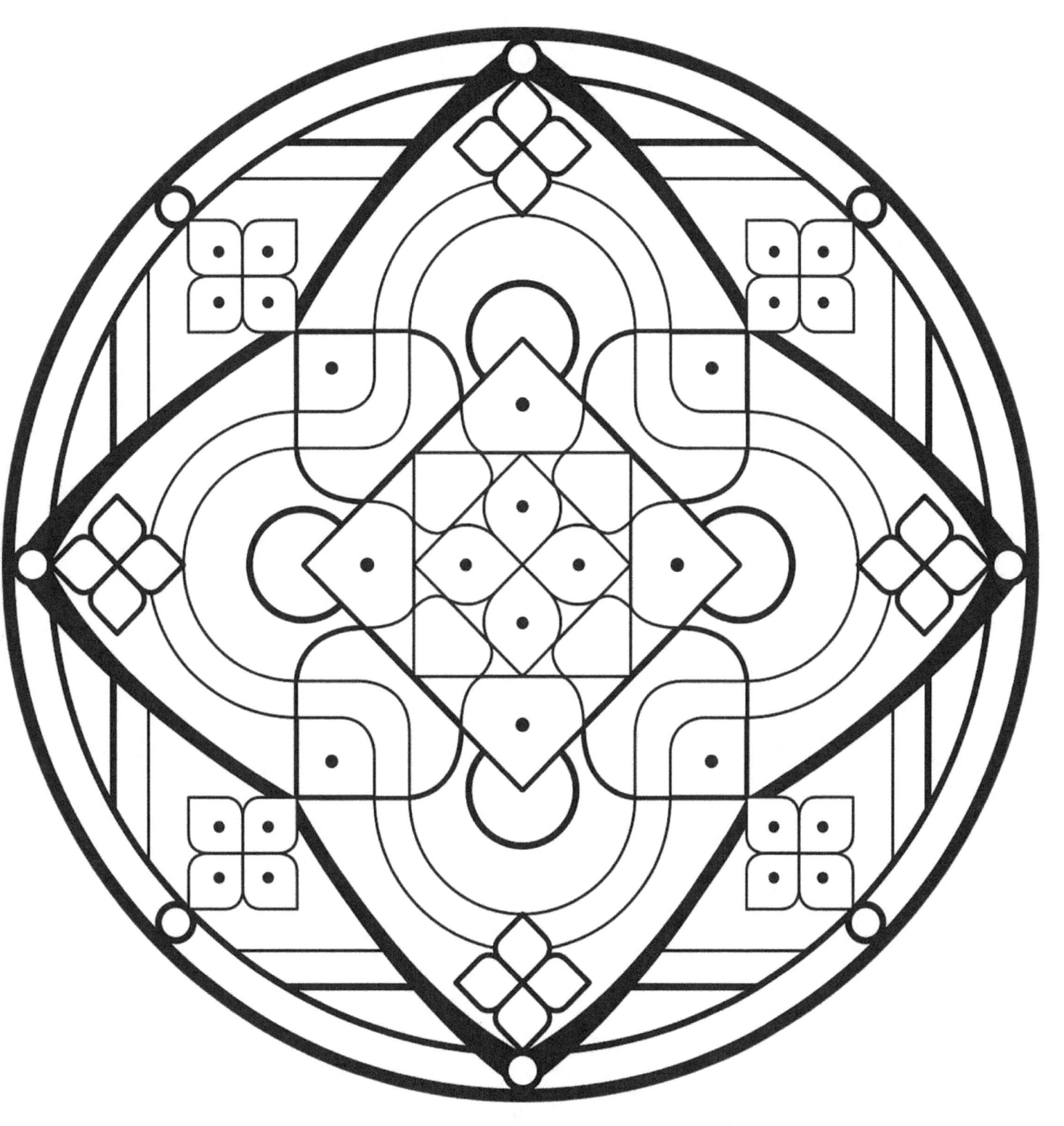

*This page intentionally left blank*

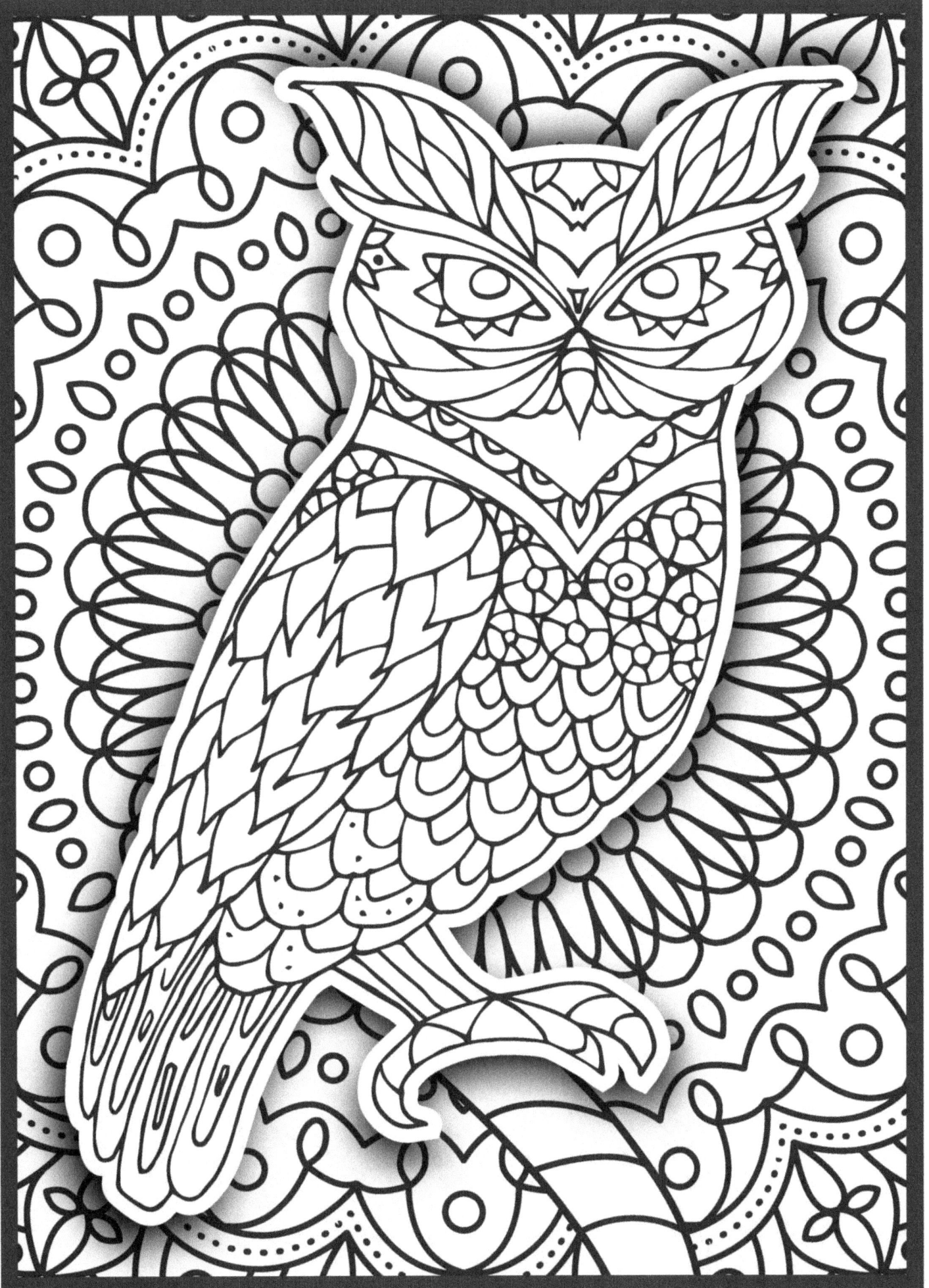

*This page intentionally left blank*

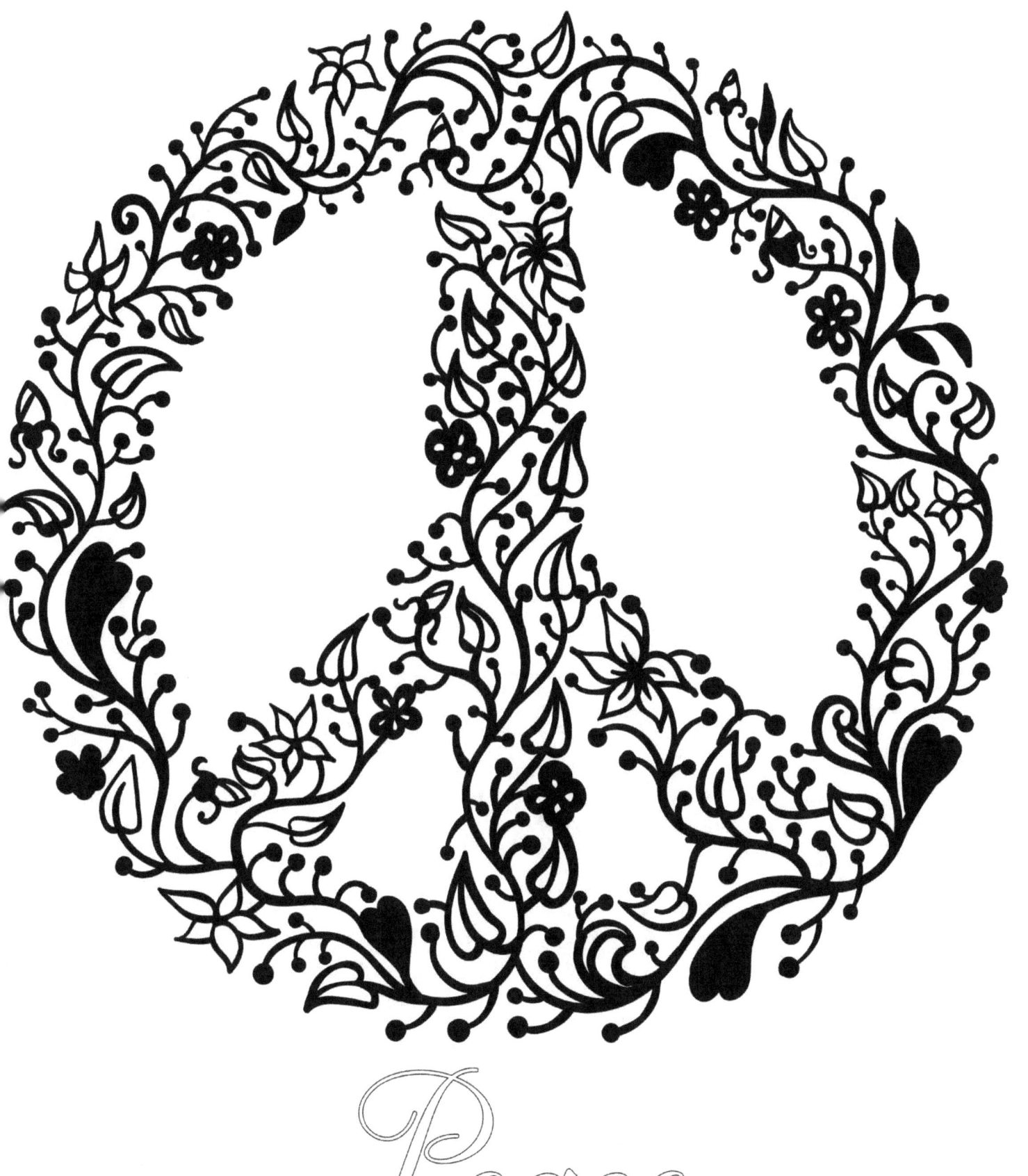

*This page intentionally left blank*

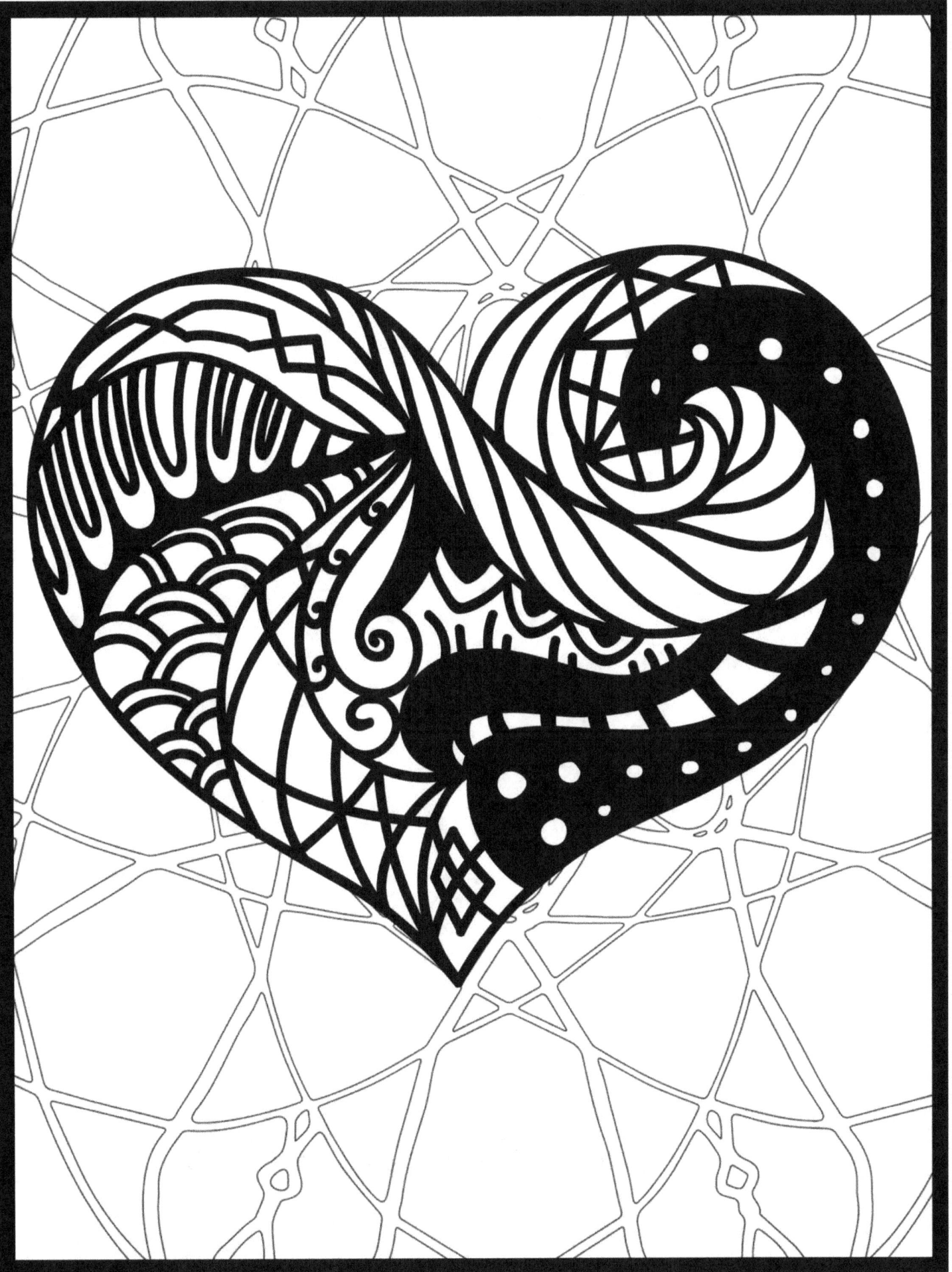

*This page intentionally left blank*

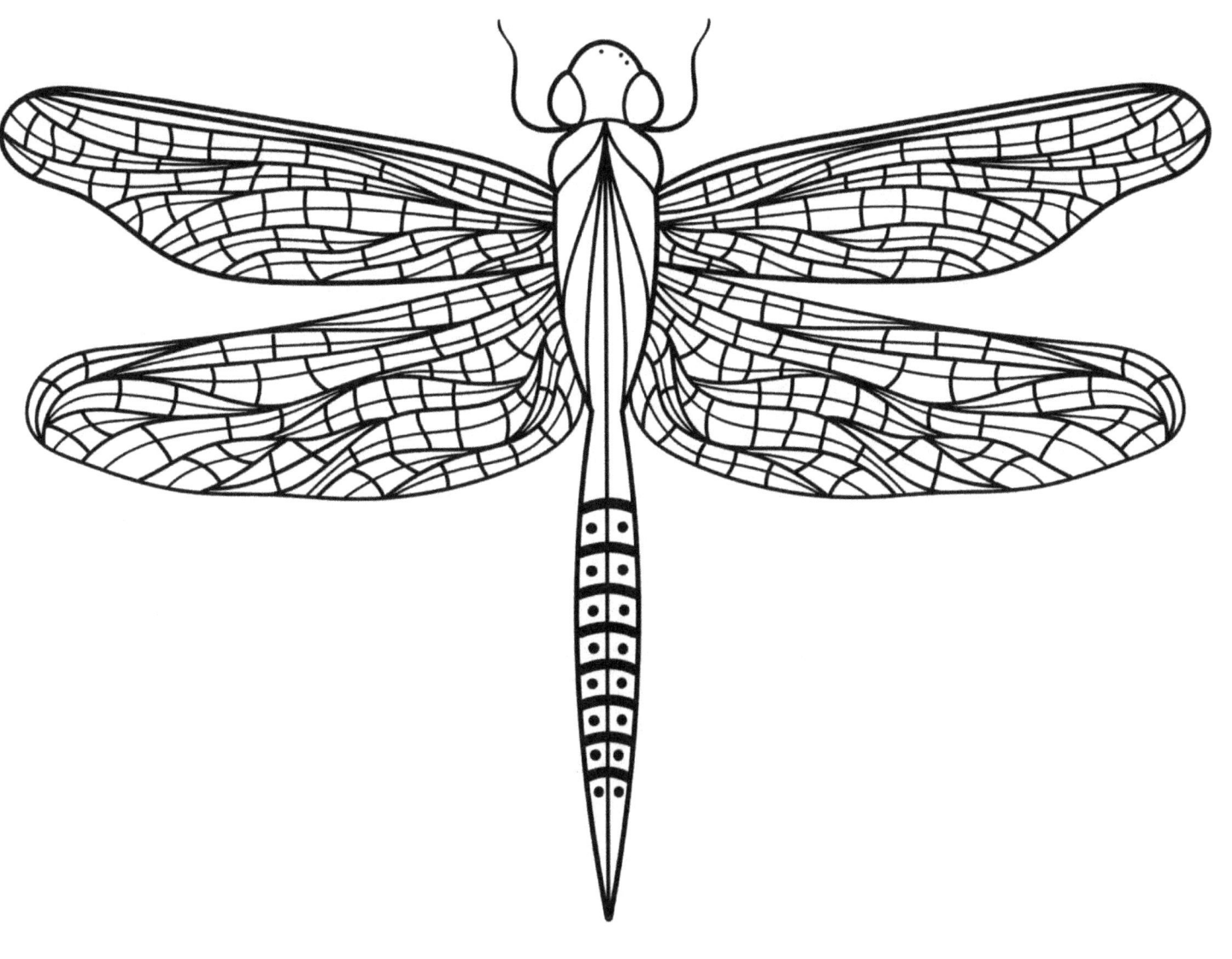

*This page intentionally left blank*

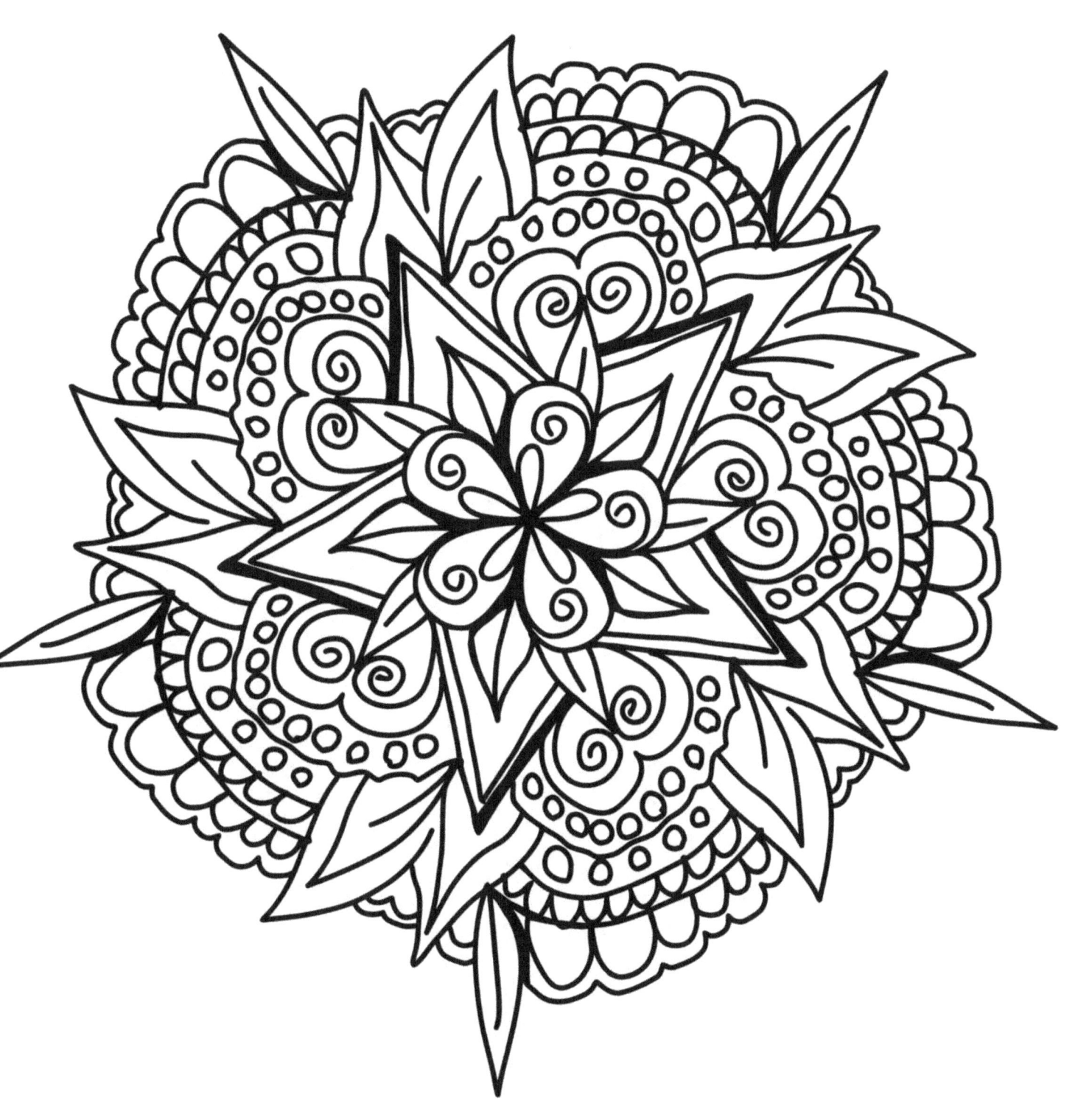

*This page intentionally left blank*

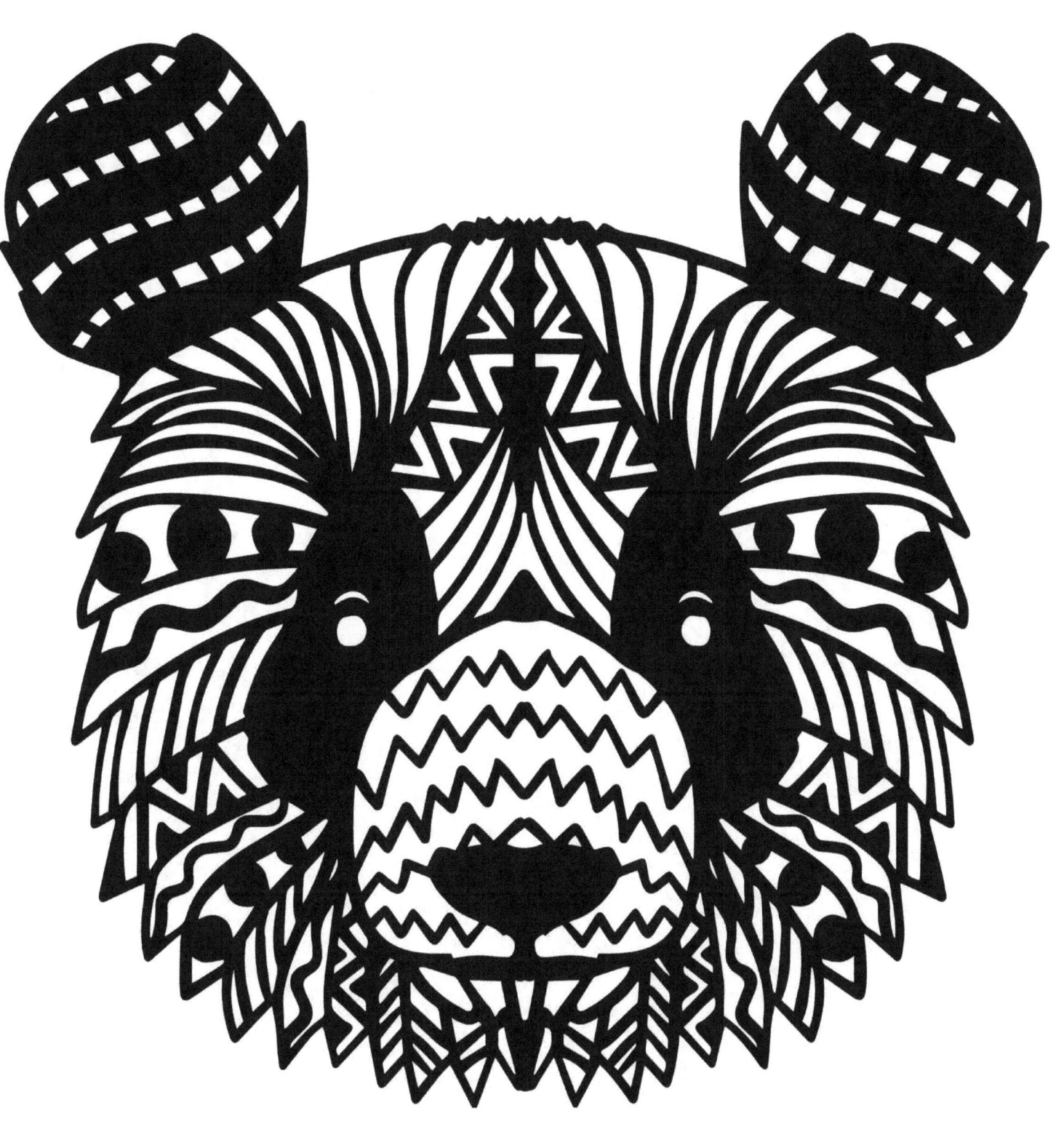

*This page intentionally left blank*

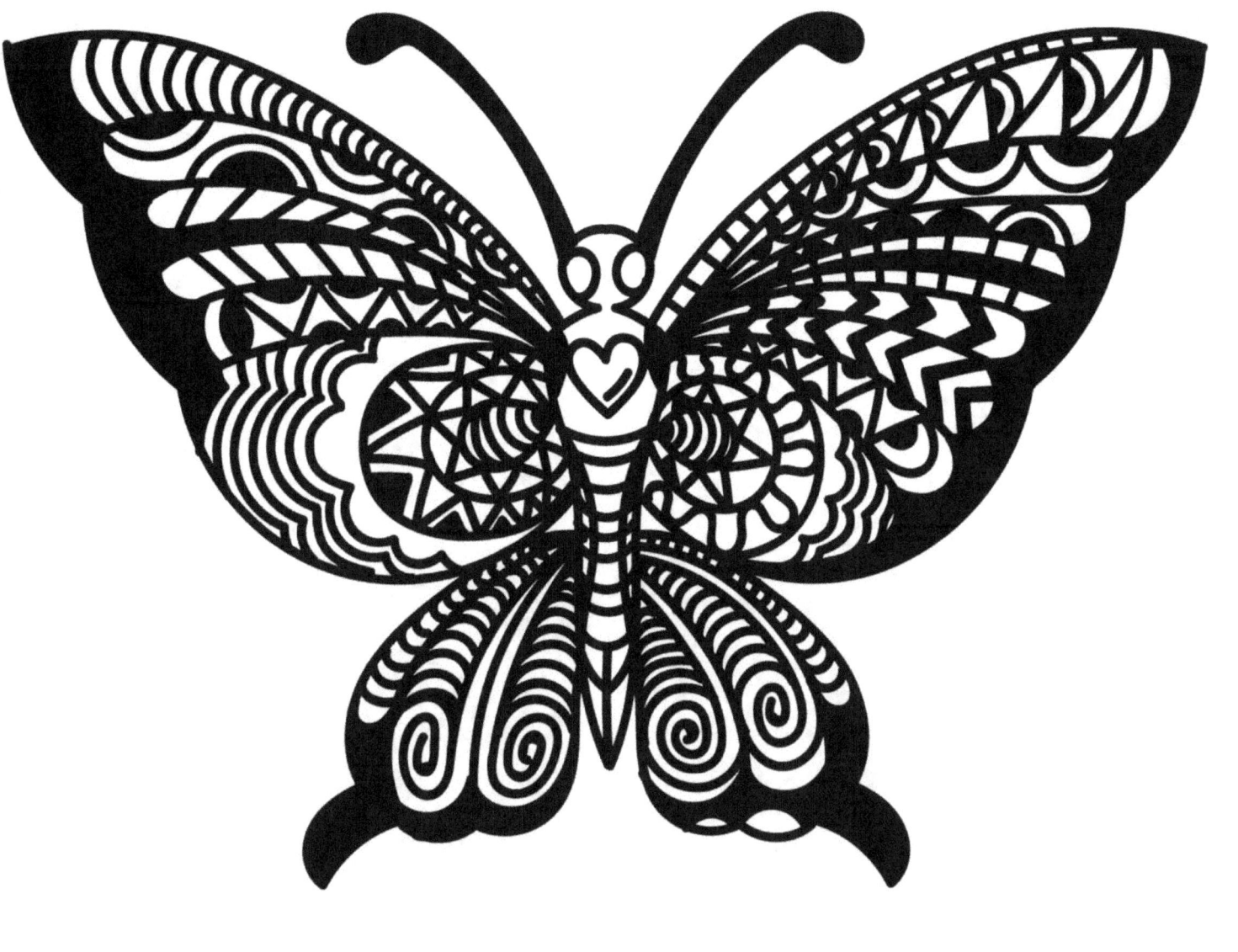

Butterfly

*This page intentionally left blank*

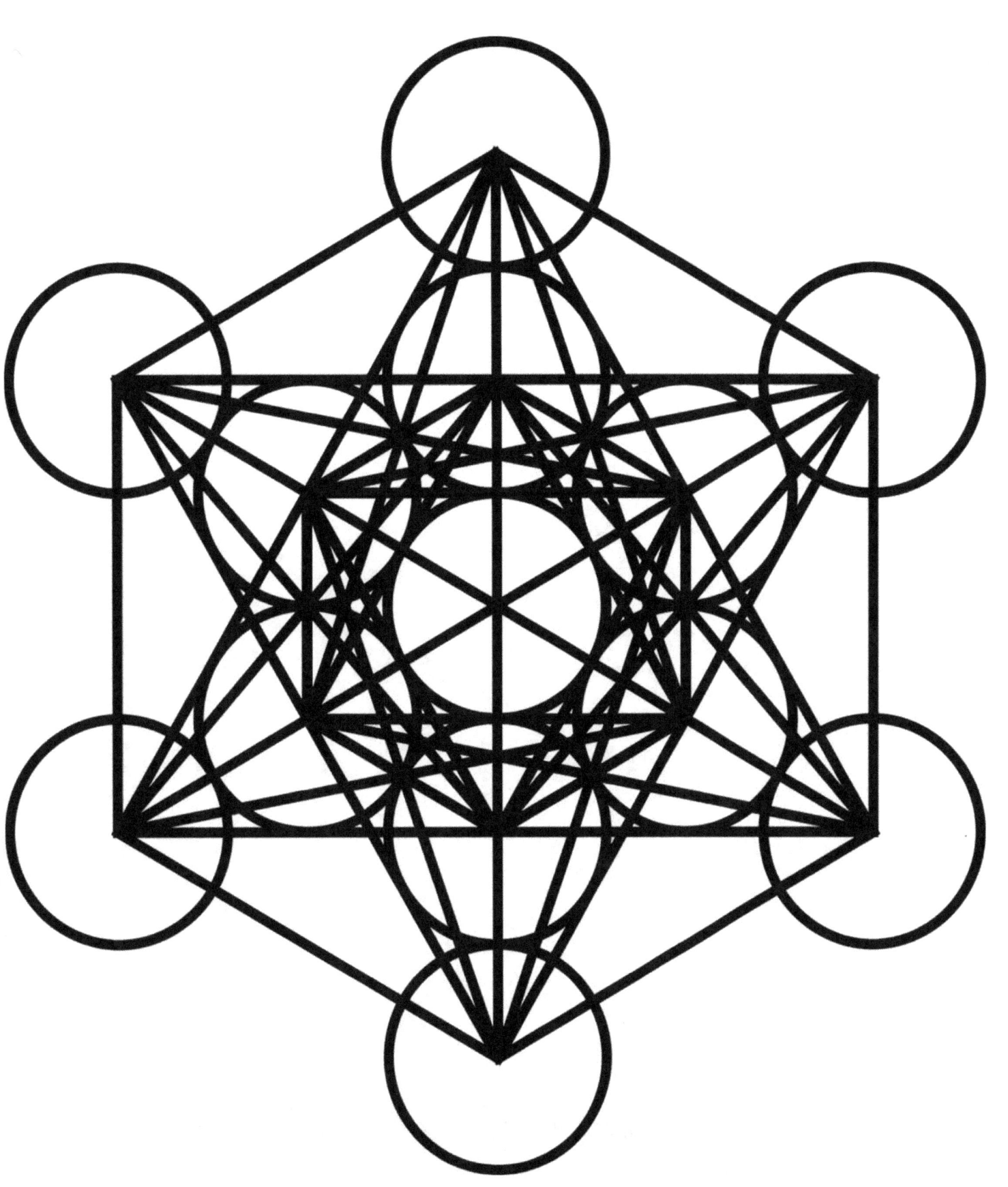

*This page intentionally left blank*

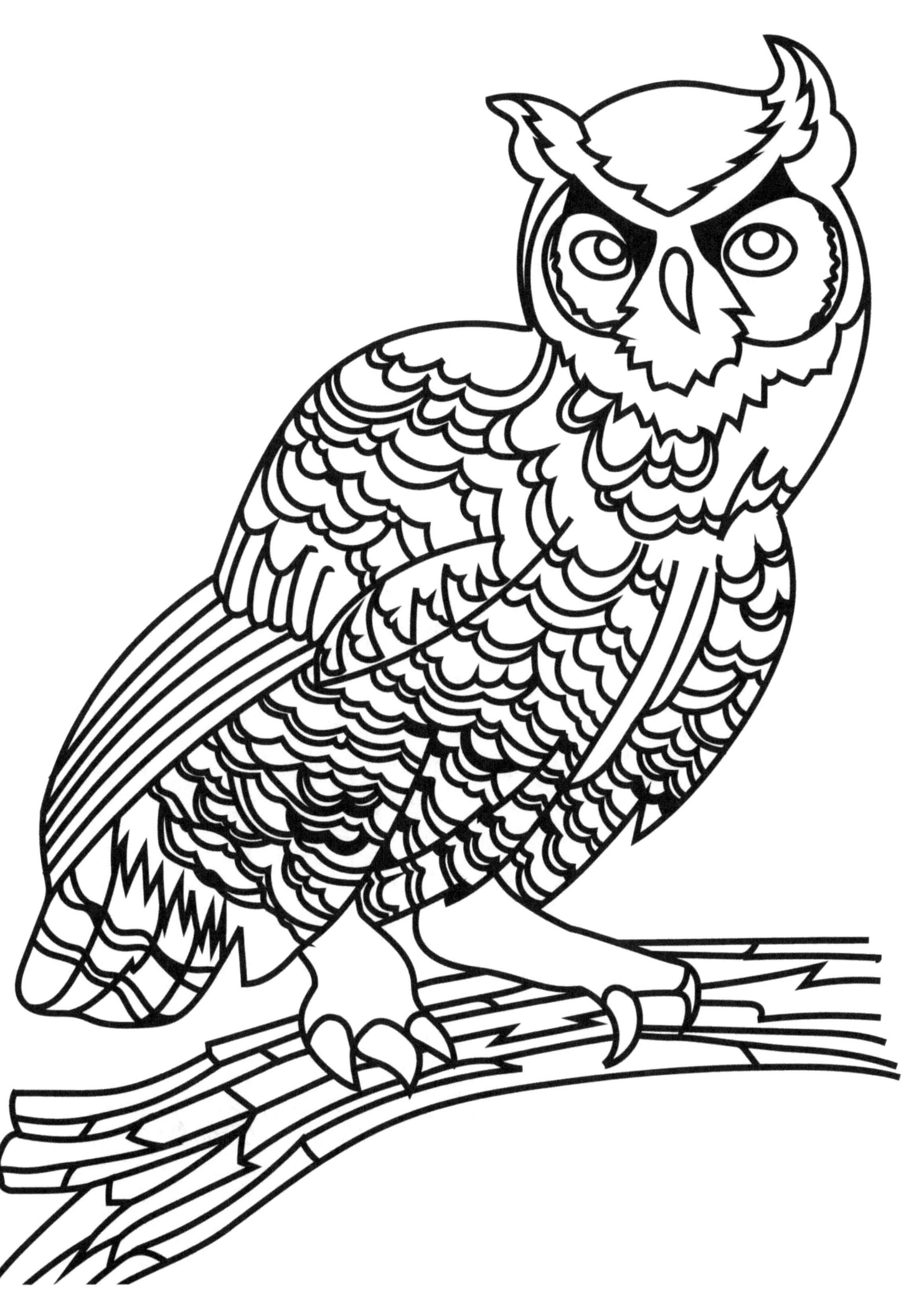

*This page intentionally left blank*

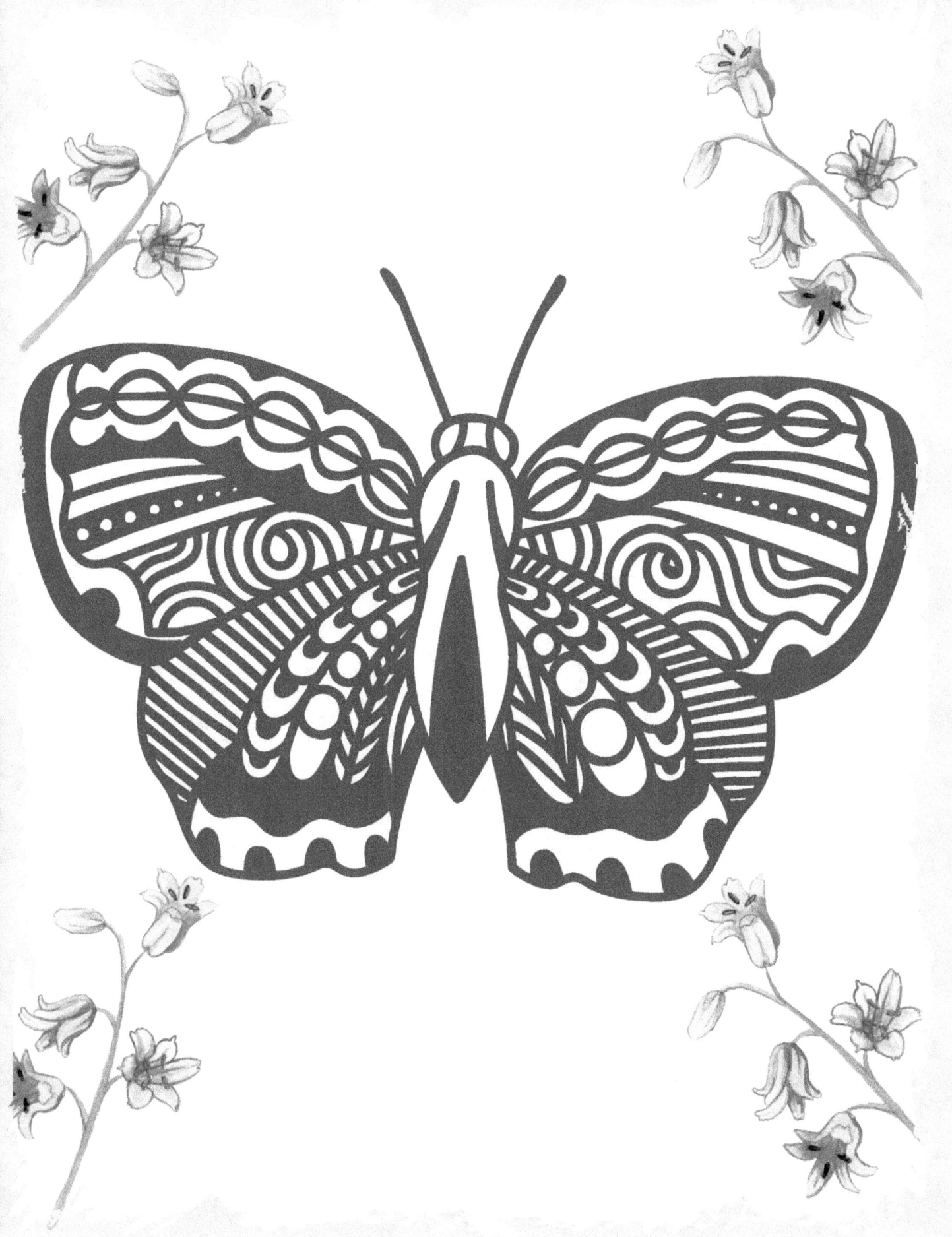

*This page intentionally left blank*

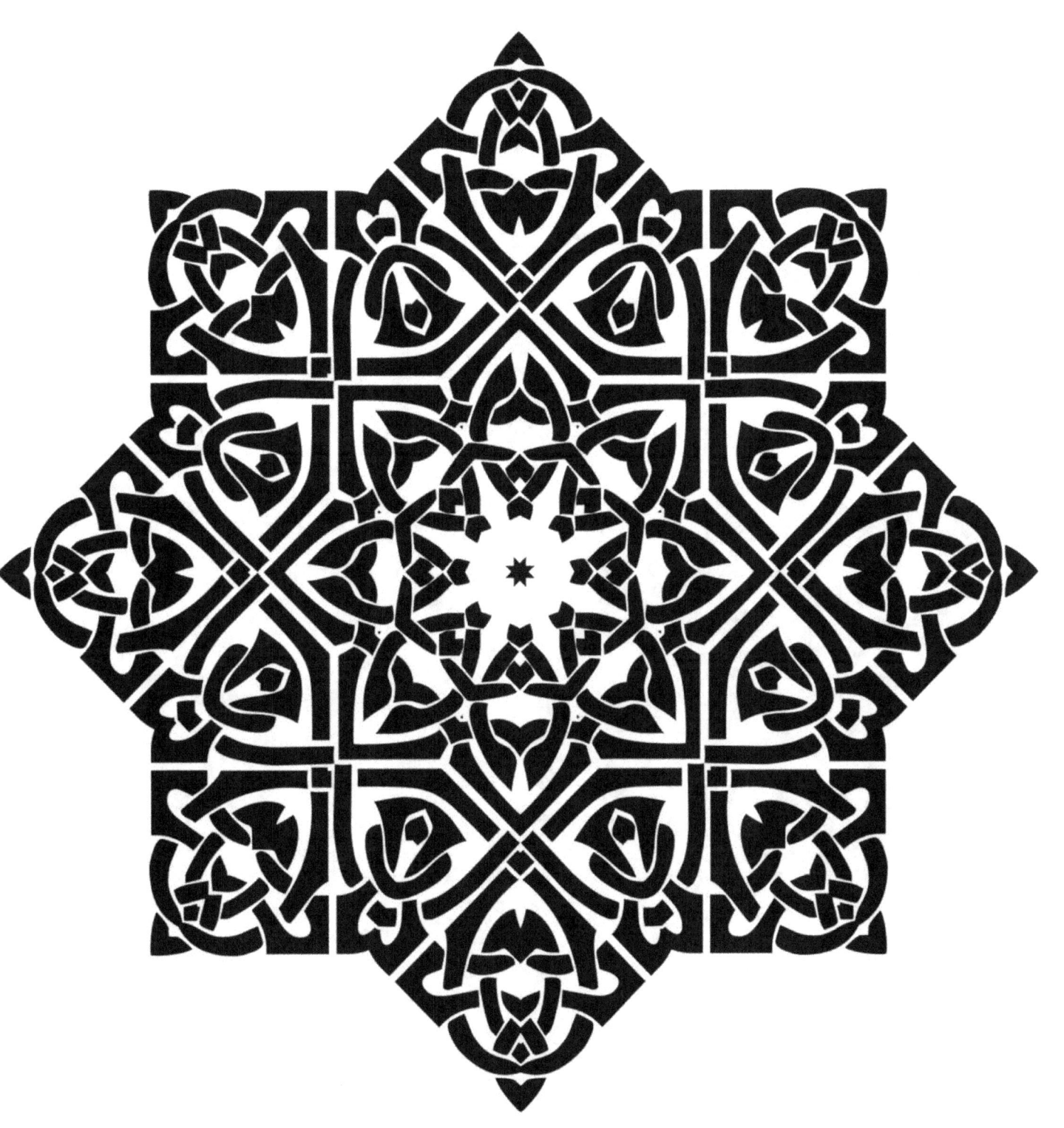

*This page intentionally left blank*

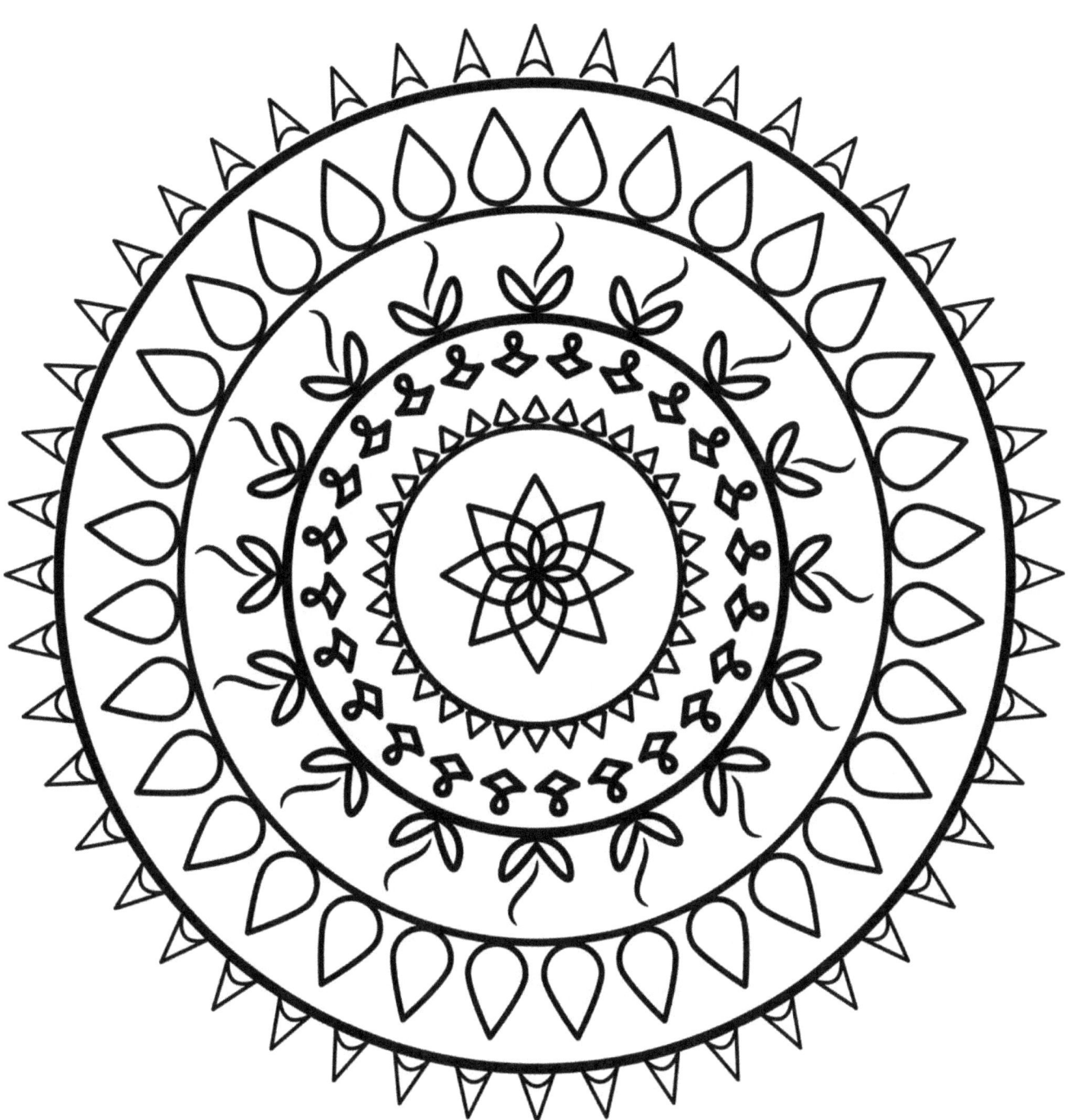

*This page intentionally left blank*

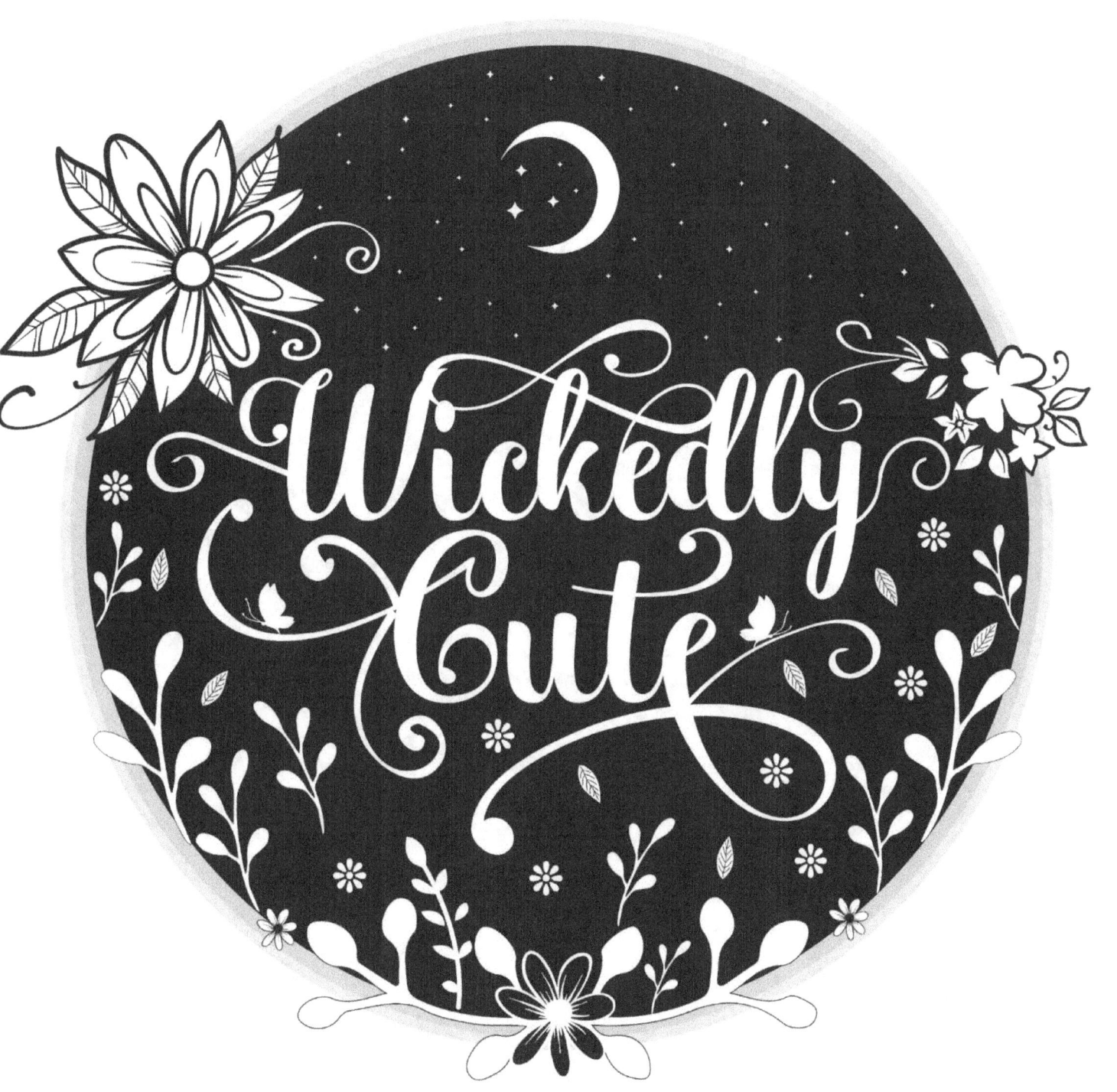

*This page intentionally left blank*

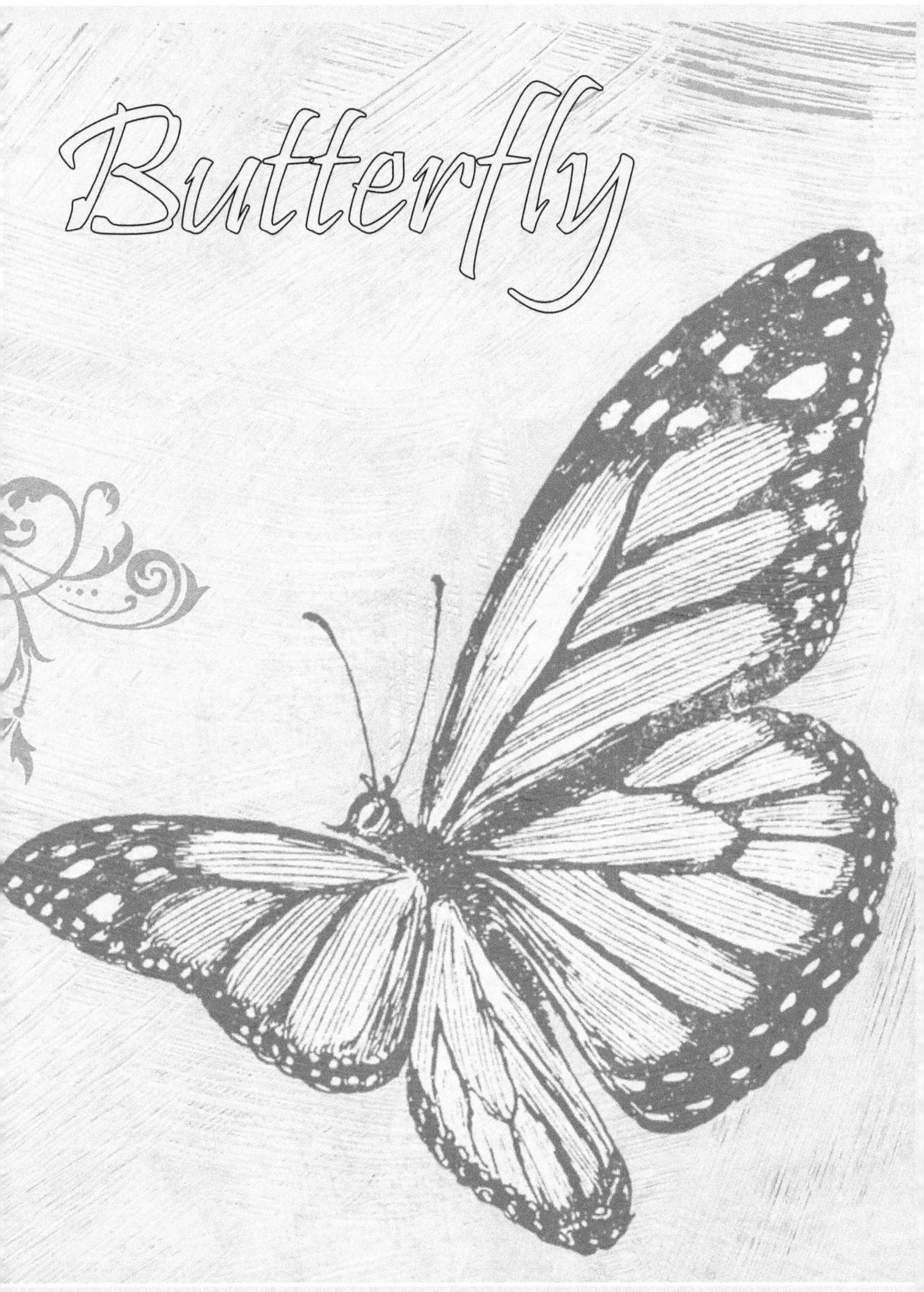

*This page intentionally left blank*

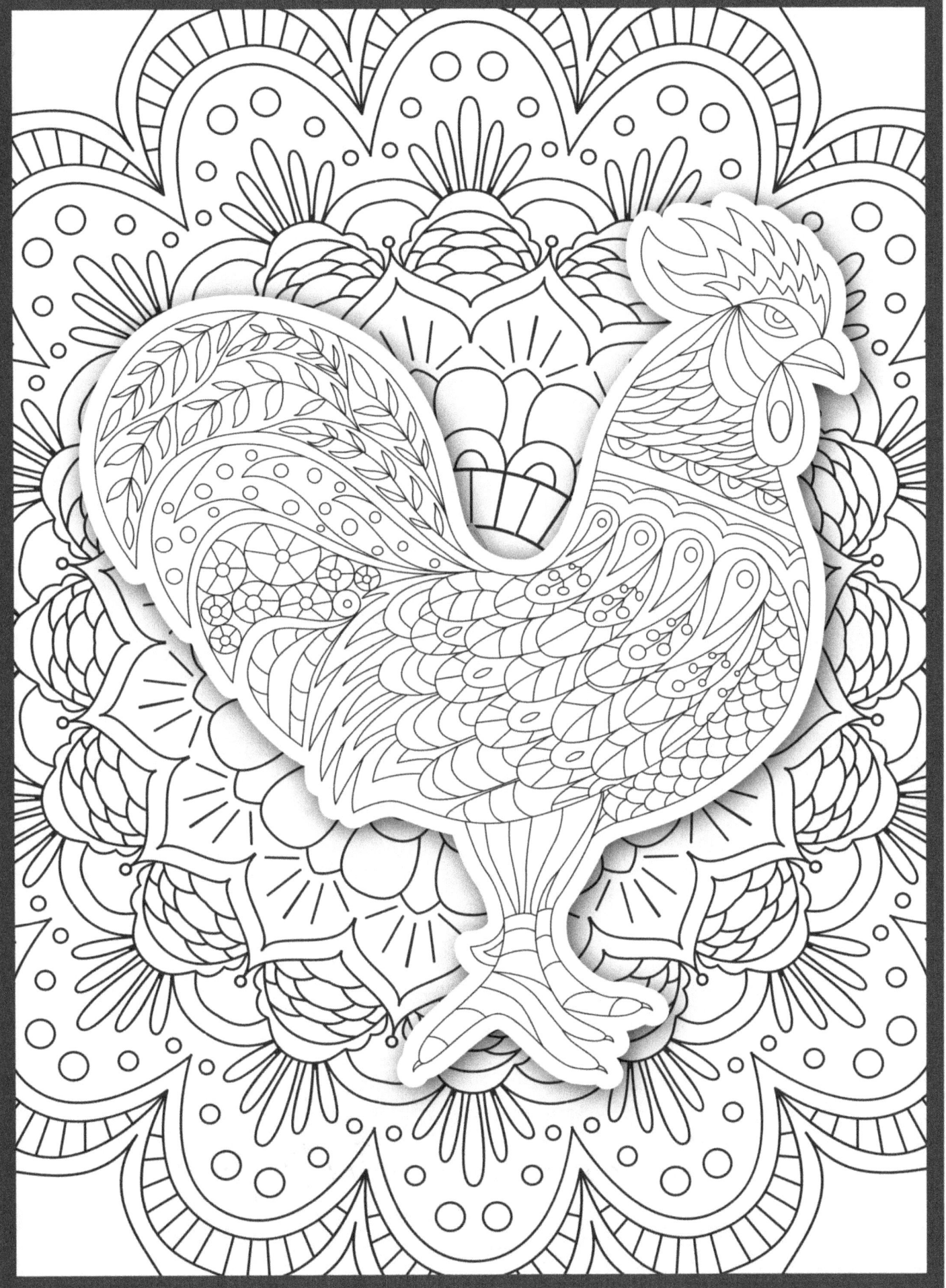

*This page intentionally left blank*

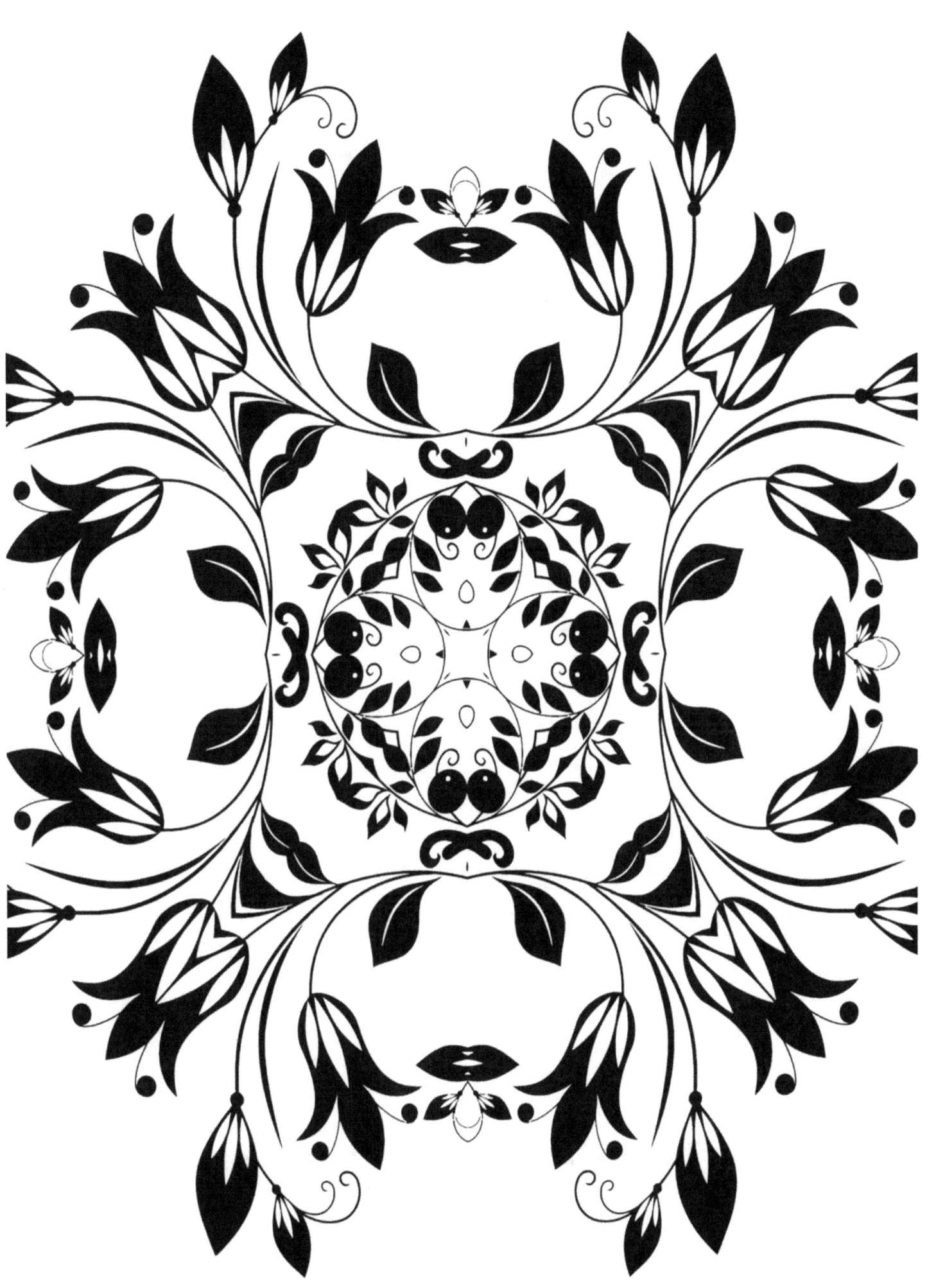

*This page intentionally left blank*

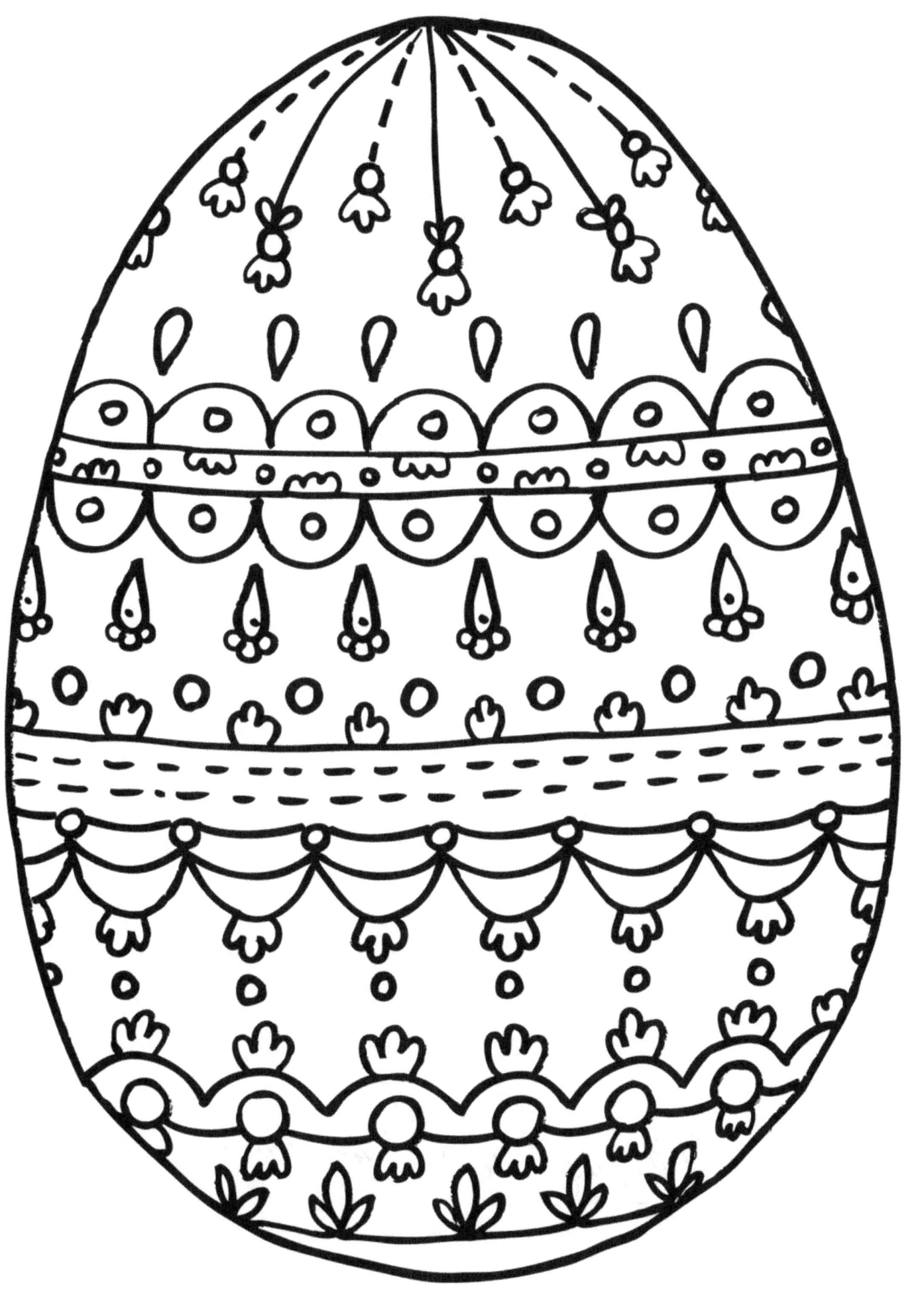

*This page intentionally left blank*

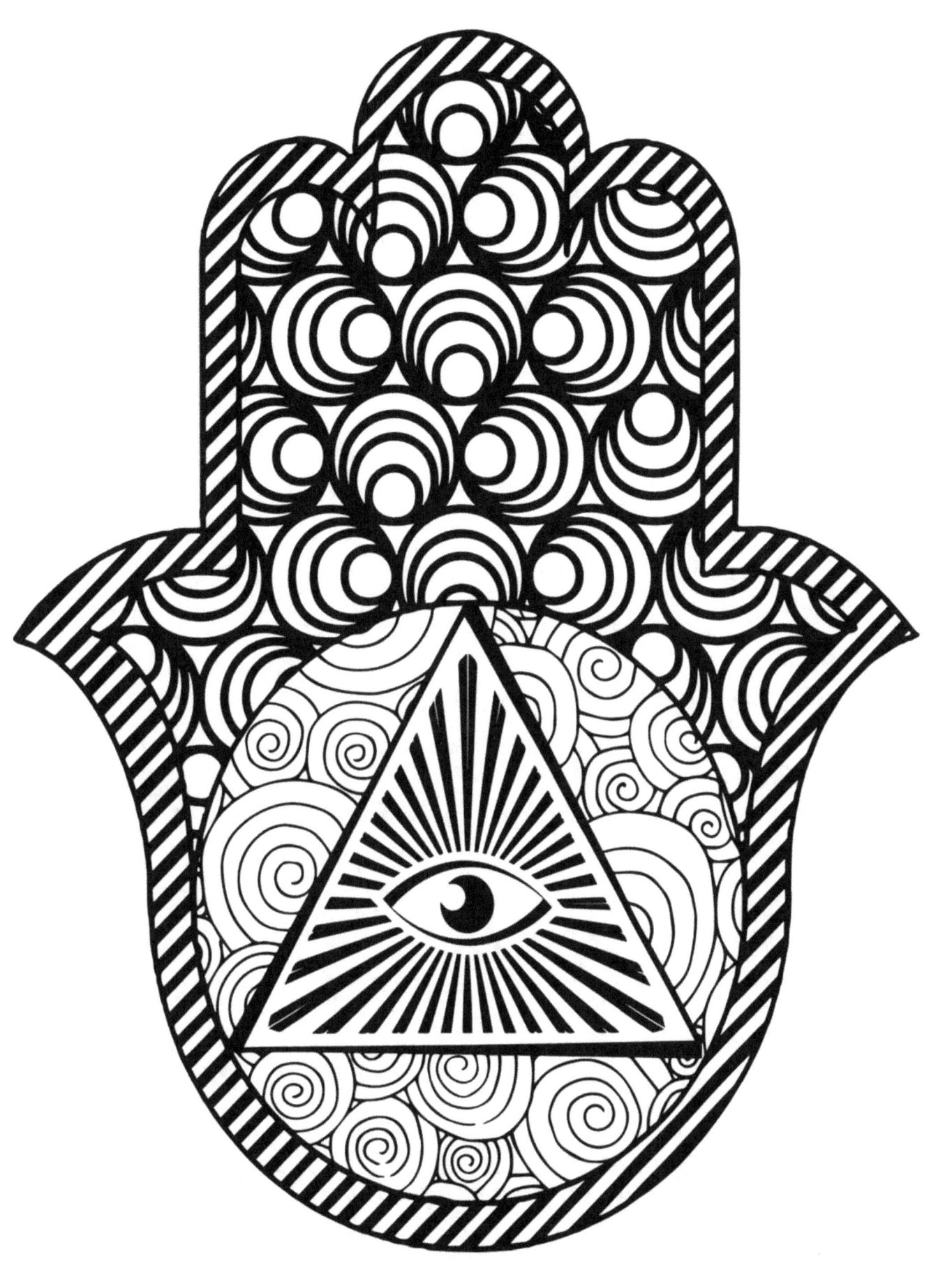

*This page intentionally left blank*

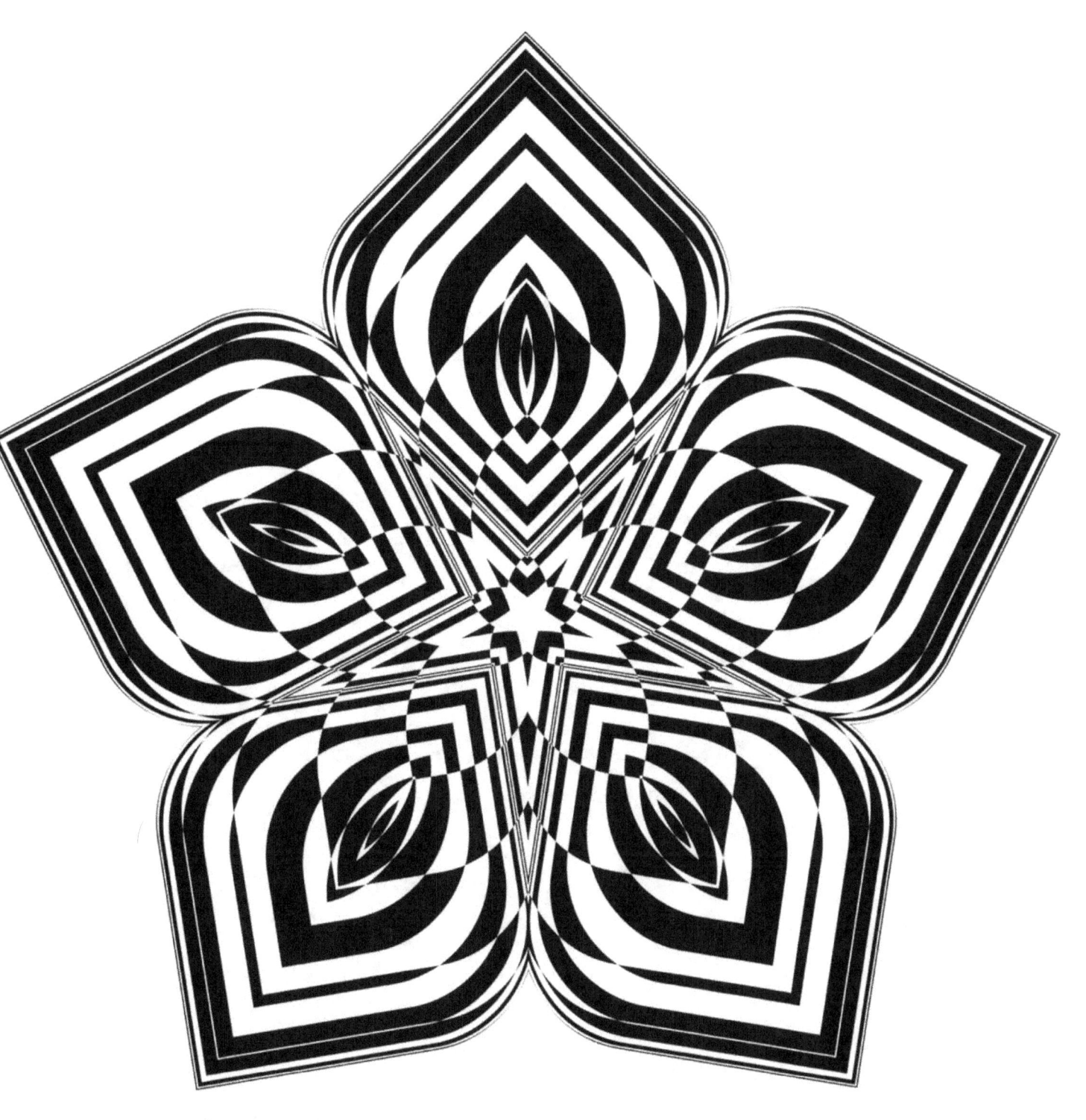

*This page intentionally left blank*

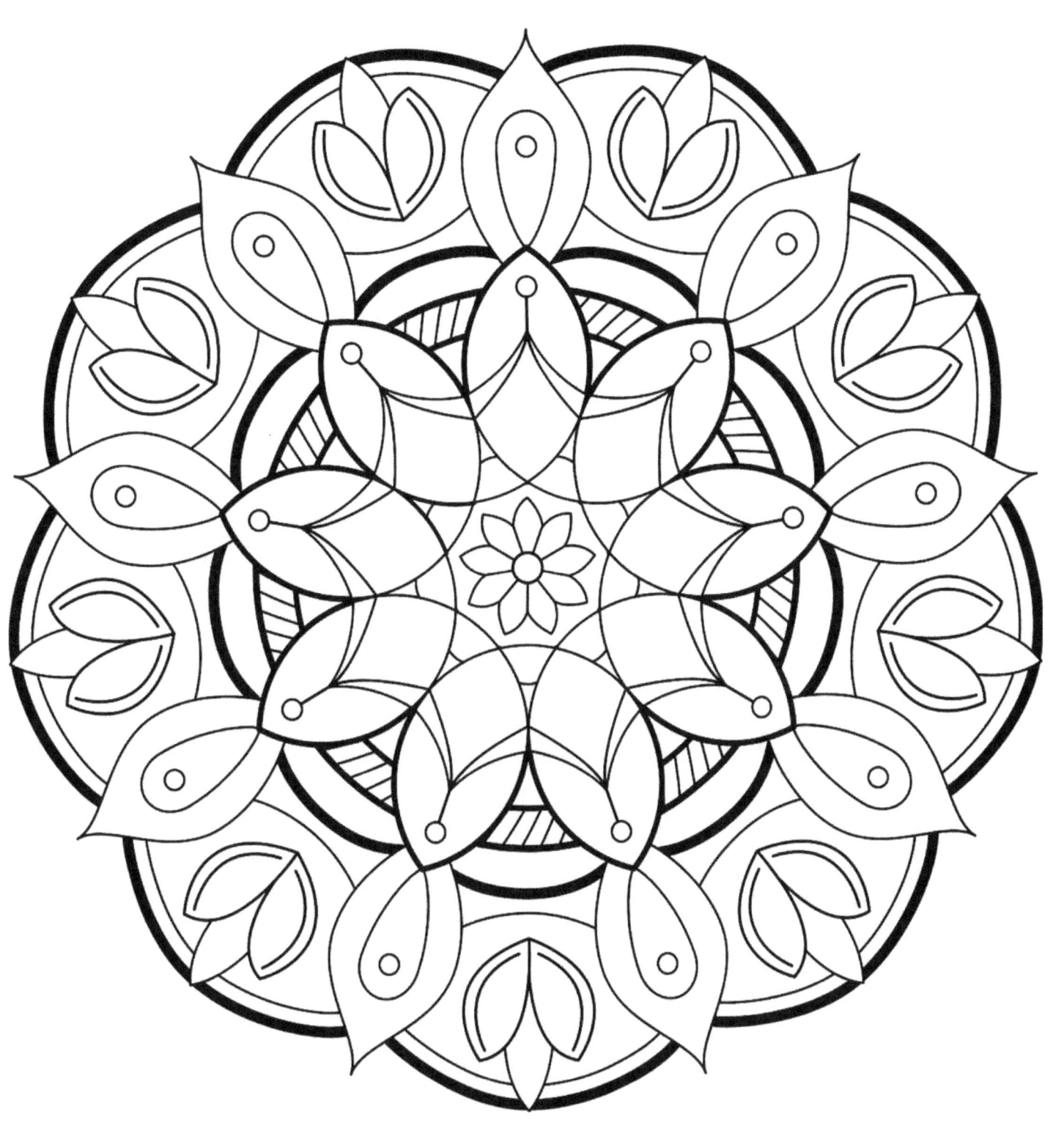

*This page intentionally left blank*

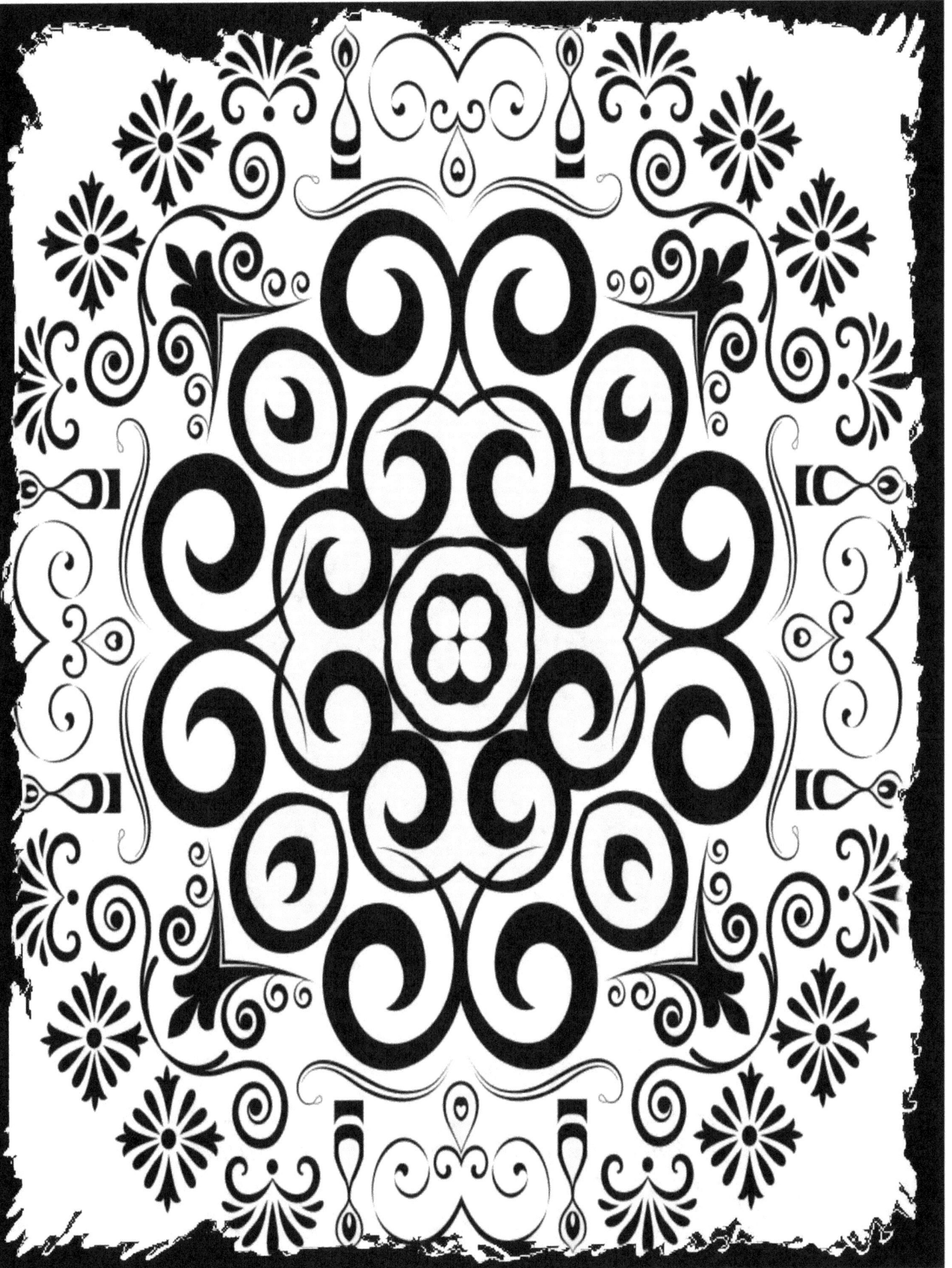

*This page intentionally left blank*

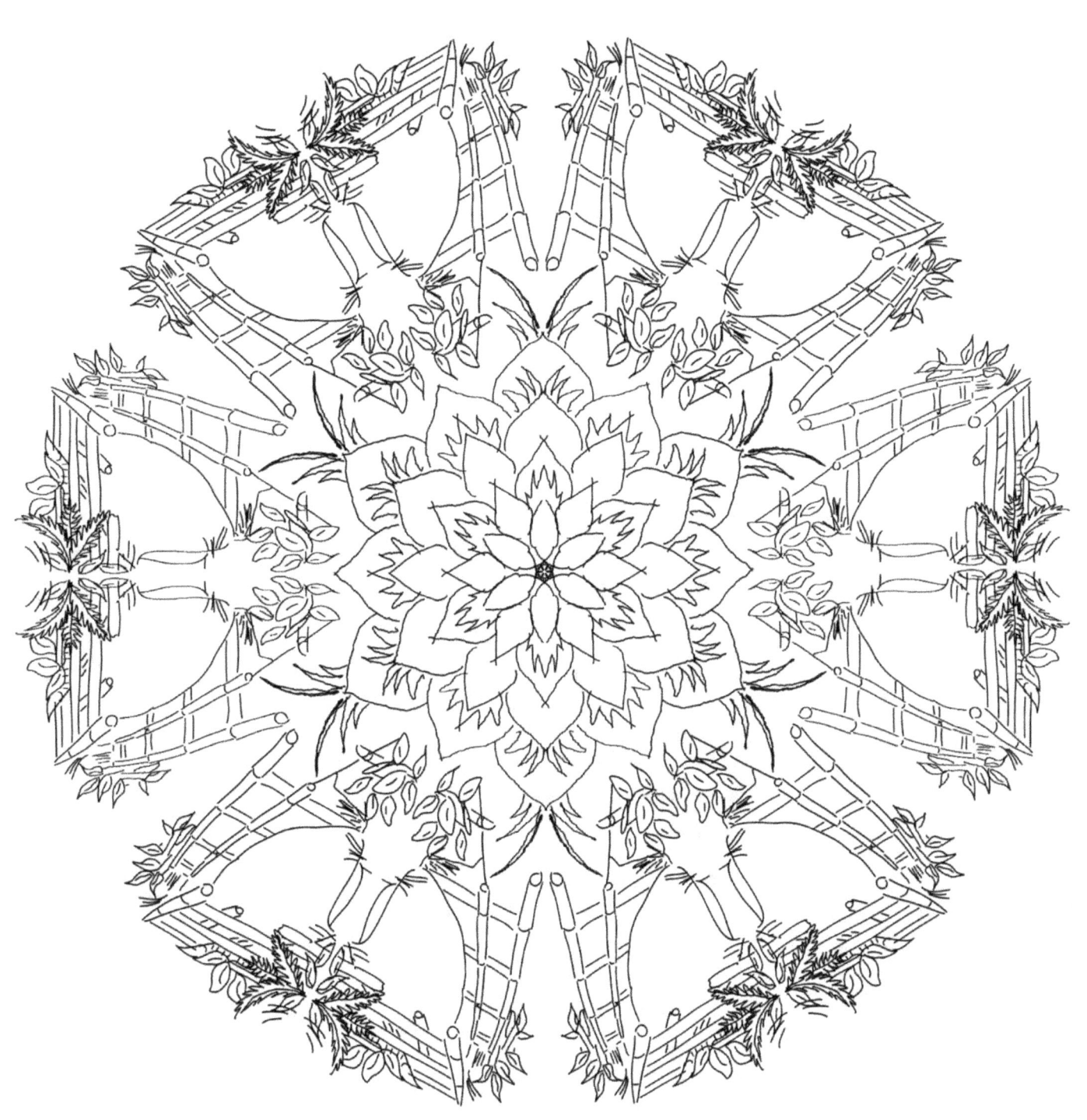

*This page intentionally left blank*

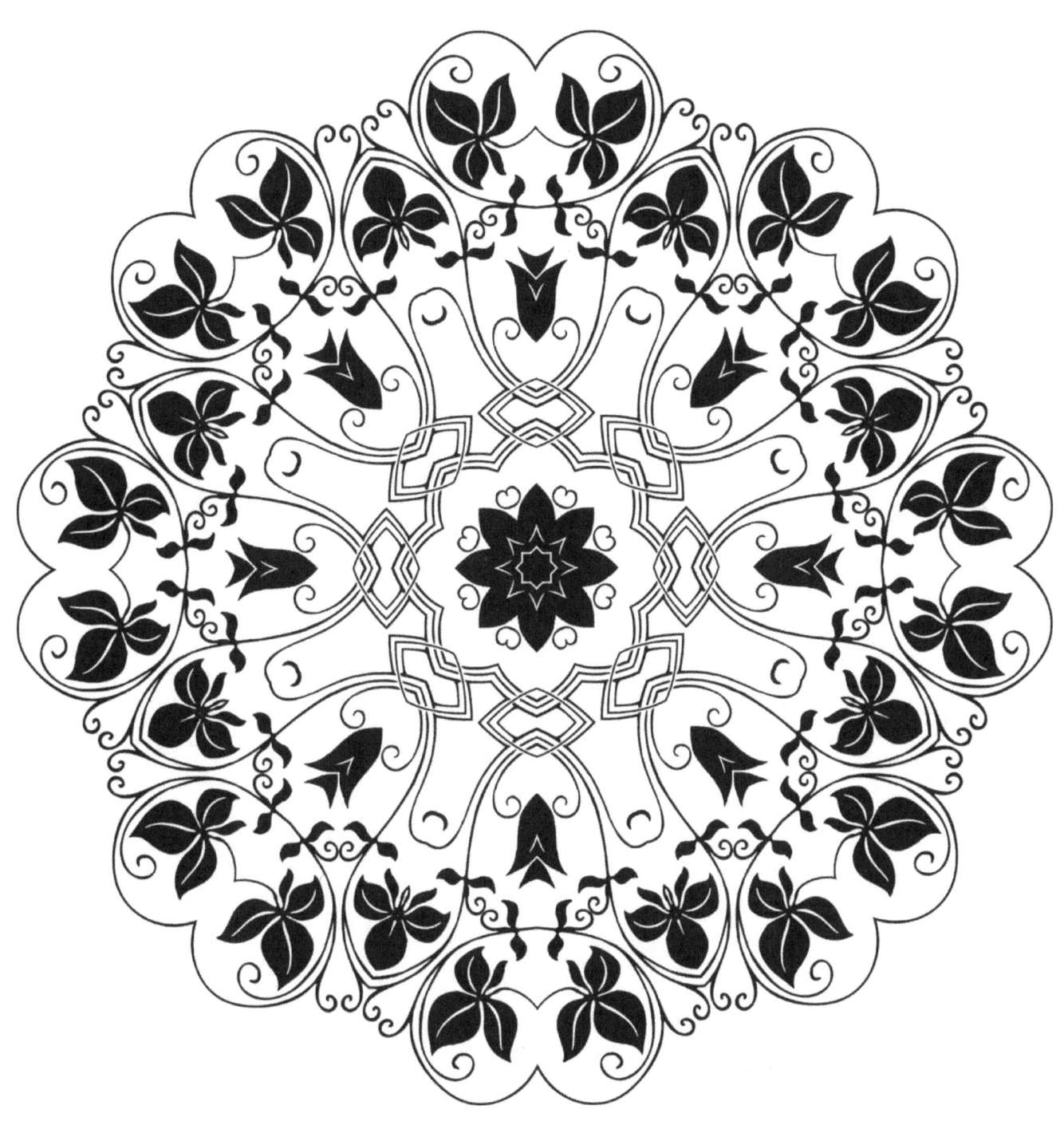

*This page intentionally left blank*

www.ingramcontent.com/pod-product-compliance
Lightning Source LLC
Chambersburg PA
CBHW060435220526
45465CB00008B/3145